Embroidered with White

The 18th century fashion for Dresden lace and other whiteworked accessories

by Heather Toomer

with drawings and patterns by Elspeth Reed

Contents

Abbreviations used in this book:

Hampshire Museums - *Hampshire County Council Museums and Archives Service*; N.T. - *The National Trust for England and Wales*
V&A - *Victoria & Albert Museum, London;* Diderot's Encyclopedia - *'Encyclopédie ou Dictionnaire raisonné des Sciences, des Arts et des Métiers' by Denis Diderot and Jean Lerond d'Alembert, 1751.*

Measurements *(all maximum unless otherwise stated)*
CB – *centre back;* D – *depth;* L – *length;* Ls – *length of side;* Lc – *length at centre;* W – *width;* Pr – *pattern repeat.*
All patterns are drawn on 1/8in squares to a scale of 1/8in = 1in

Acknowledgments

We are extremely grateful to all the museum staff involved in this task for their willing and patient help and encouragement over several years. In particular we must mention Alison Carter, Sarah Howard and Sue Washington (Hampshire Museums), Julia Fox (Devonshire Collection of Period Costume), Miles Lambert (Gallery of Costume, Manchester), Frances Pritchard (Whitworth Art Gallery), Catherine Littlejohn (Blaise Castle House Museum), Jeremy Farrell (Museum of Costume and Textiles, Nottingham), Grace Evans (Chertsey Museum), Althea McKenzie (Hereford Museum and Art Gallery), Amanda Draper (Harris Museum and Art Gallery), Shelley Tobin (Exeter Museums), Georges Potirakis (Wimpole Hall, N.T.), Gail Marsh (R. B. Kay-Shuttleworth Collection), Mary Alexander (Guildford Museum), Linda Wicks (Carrow House Costume and Textile Study Centre, Norwich), Polly Putnam (Temple Newsam, Leeds), Janine Derbyshire (Pickford House Museum, Derby), Pat Perryman (Allhallows Museum, Honiton), Pauline Rushton (Walker Museum and Art Gallery), Moira Thunder and Susan North (V&A).

We also express our thanks to the following institutions for their kind permission to study and photograph articles in their collections and/or to reproduce them:

Allhallows Museum, Honiton: *Plates IV.34, 37, 49, 50*
Blaise Castle House Museum, Bristol: *Plates: II.50; IV.5, 21*
Boston Museum of Fine Arts, Boston, Massachusetts. USA: *Plates: II.13, 52*
Bridgeman Art Library: *Plate II.31*
Bristol University Library: *Plates: I.2, 3; II.84; IV.45*
Cavalcade of Costume, Blandford Forum: *Plates II. 81,a,b*
Devonshire Collection of Period Costume, Totnes: *Plates II.2b, 51, 56, 64*
English Heritage (Iveagh Bequest): *Plate II.57*
Exeter University Library: *Plate: II.74*

Guildford Museum: *Plate III.7*
Hampshire County Council Museums & Archives Service: *Plates II.17, 18, 20, 77, 79*
Harris Museum & Art Gallery, Preston: *Plates II.1, 78; III.2,a,b*
Hereford Museum & Art Gallery: *Plates II.10, 12, 15, 19, 34*
Manchester City Galleries: *Plate III.13*
Mapledurham Trust: *Plate II.44, front cover*
Norfolk Museums & Archaeology Service (Carrow House Costume & Textile Study Centre): *Plates III.12; IV.2,a-d*
National Museums of Northern Ireland: *Plates II.59*
Nottingham Museum of Costume & Textiles: *Plates II.30; III.5; IV.4, 20,a, 21*
N.T., Wimpole Hall: *Plate II.68,69*
Pickford House Museum, Derby: *Plates II.11; IV.40,a*
Rachel B. Kay-Shuttleworth Collection, Gawthorpe Hall: *Plates III.16; IV.38,a*
V&A: *Plates II.8, 26, 27, 32, 35, 53, 67; III.8, 9, 10, 11*
Witt Library, The Courtauld Institute of Art: *Plates I.1; II.47, 65*

We should also like to thank the Costume Society and the Southern Counties Costume Society for their bursaries towards reproduction fees and travelling expenses for our research.

Very special thanks are also due to Rosemary Baker, Julia Craig, Alan and Vanessa Hopkins, Harry Matthews, Ann Pilling and Anne Swift for allowing us to borrow, pattern and photograph articles from their collections and to Richard Davin for reading and advising on the draft. Last, but not least, thanks are due to our husbands Clive Toomer and Martin Reed for their forbearance and encouragement throughout and particularly to Clive Toomer for proof-reading at various stages of the work.

Preface

My primary collection has always been lace but whitework crept in at an early stage. It has a similar aesthetic appeal: it relies for its effect on nuances of light, shade and texture and has a purity lacking in coloured fabrics.

My first purchase came by chance. The contents of a minor stately home in Cornwall were for sale and, in among the odds and ends in a back room, was a tin box full of lace and whitework. My prize cost less than fifty pounds, a mere bagatelle to an euphoric group of auctioneers who had raised millions from the sale of fine portraits, furniture, silver etc., but the contents, though much worn, torn and re-used, reflected the status that the owners of the house once had. There was my first 17th-century Venetian needlepoint, fine Flemish bobbin laces and other samples too numerous to list. Though not in themselves valuable, they were a great help to me in learning about lace.

In amongst them was a corner and edging which I later recognised to be part of an 18th-century whiteworked handkerchief – I use that term in the 18th-century sense of a large square which, when folded into a triangle, would have been worn around the shoulders. The work was incredibly fine, of the type known as 'Dresden lace' although it is truly an embroidery. Gradually I added aprons, complete handkerchiefs and sleeve ruffles to the collection but realised how little I knew about them. Although lace was reasonably well understood and many lace and embroidery books illustrated examples of whitework, few dealt with it in any depth. I determined to redress the balance and soon realised why so little had been written on the subject: there is very little evidence by way of dated examples or illustrations to enable a comprehensive chronology of the changes in embroidery styles and uses through the 18th century to be built up and even less evidence to link surviving examples to specific places of manufacture.

The following text does not, therefore, pretend to answer all the questions about this little-known area of the textile world but will, I hope, inspire others to look at whitework afresh and perhaps, at some stage, fill in further gaps in its history.

Introduction

As the title of this book suggests, it is concerned with white embroideries and, more specifically, those used on costume accessories in the 18th century. It is thus concerned with decorative accessories: not the maid's plain, utilitarian apron but aprons and kerchiefs decorated with fine white embroidery, worn more for show than utility.

During our period these were worn widely in Britain by women with sufficient wealth to indulge in finery. Along with aprons and kerchiefs there were flowing sleeve ruffles and, later, shawls. The more expensive accessories were in fine, often diaphanous, cottons or lawns on which even the slight changes in density created by white embroidery made sufficient contrast to be visible over coloured dress fabrics. At the same time, women's stomachers were sometimes embroidered in white but in rather different techniques: their lining precluded transparency and therefore quilting and raised surface work achieved the desired decorative effects. Some men's waistcoats were similarly treated and, although such an essential part of men's dress in the 18th century cannot be considered an accessory, a few are included here as examples of this different aspect of embroidery. For similar reasons a few silk garments with self-coloured decoration are introduced.

Caps also featured largely in women's wardrobes in the 18th century but the few surviving examples I have seen do not allow me to do justice to the wealth of styles shown in illustrations of the period. Apart from a few lappets and cap backs, therefore, headwear is left for another occasion.

Towards the end of our period a rather different accessory, the chemisette, or habit shirt as it was then more generally known, came into use: it filled in a low neckline instead of, or as well as, a kerchief. Habit shirts could be included in this work but they start a new story and are left for another book. Pockets and sewing bags used to carry a woman's necessities are, however, included.

Examples of all these articles are to be found in British costume collections, both public and private, and it is with the British social scene that this book is largely concerned.

Although our fashions went through very similar changes to those in continental Europe and we imported much of the finest whitework, particularly from Germany, there were differences some of which, I hope, will become apparent in the following pages.

Plate I.1 *Detail from a portrait of a family group, by Gawen Hamilton; c1730s. (©Witt Library, The Courtauld Institute of Art, London)*

Portraits showing family groups engaged in some form of activity, whether indoors or out, survive in great numbers from the 18th century and show typical informal dress of their periods. Here the ladies wear long, fitted gowns with elbow-length sleeves. The seated lady also wears a white kerchief round her neckline and a long white apron: these, together with the white ruffles all the ladies wear at the elbow, constitute the main subject of this work.

Section I

WHITEWORK EMBROIDERY IN THE 18TH CENTURY

A few notes on the workers

In the 18th century hand-sewing was the order of the day: personal linen, household linen, clothing, furnishings, everything had to be hand-sewn. There were attempts to mechanise the process but these were not brought to fruition until the 19th century. The result was that most women, and some men also, spent some time every day with their needles. For the poor this might mean darning, altering and mending, cutting down worn adult clothes to make new ones for children, and generally making do with second-hand fabrics and clothing which they were given or could buy at minimum expense. Even the wealthy frequently made chemises, shirts and other items of personal clothing for themselves and their families while all who had a little leisure would use it to embellish their clothing and surroundings with embroidery.

There were also the professionals: the tailors who made men's outfits and women's tailored garments such as riding habits; the mantua makers for women's robes and petticoats; milliners for trimmings and accessories; seamstresses who did plain sewing; embroiderers skilled in working with silks and precious metal threads; and others too numerous to mention but among whom were the embroiderers in white thread on white fabrics.

Their work set them apart from the embroiderers in precious materials; the latter were highly regarded craftsmen and women whose masters, in many European countries, had or still belonged to guilds which controlled standards and generally tried to ensure that prices were maintained at reasonable levels. Whitework embroideresses, like plain seamstresses, had no such protection★. Little is known about how supply and demand were satisfied but at least some whitework was sold through milliners, haberdashers, lace dealers or other suppliers of linen goods such as the lingères in France who dealt, inter alia, in a wide variety of personal linens, such as shirts and chemises.

Some merchants certainly also organised the manufacture, taking orders from clients, whether middlemen or end users, supplying fabrics and designs to the workers and taking in the finished work for onward sale. Little trace has been left of the workers themselves; their hours of work were no doubt long, as were those of all manual workers; their pay was no doubt low as they had no supporting organisation to fight for increases; their working conditions were no doubt poor as most of them would have been outworkers, living in tenements or cottages. Were it not for the beautiful, surviving products of their labour, we would have little evidence that they ever existed.

★ The entry under 'BRODEUR' in Diderot's Encyclopedia states 'Brodeur est l'ouvrier qui orde les étoffes d'ouvrages de broderie. Les Brodeurs, à Paris, font communauté. L on ne comprend sous le nom de Brodeurs que les ouvriers qui travailles sur les étoffes. Les broderies en linge se font par des femmes qui ne sont ni du corps des Brodeurs ni d'aucun d'autre.' *(It is the manufacturer who orders the fabrics for works of embroidery. The embroidery manufacturers in Paris form a guild. Only the manufacturers who work on silks are included under the name 'embroiderers'. Embroideries on linen are carried out by women who are neither members of the Guild of Embroiderers nor of any other.)*

THE BASIC PRODUCTION METHODS

Frames and supports

With so little documentation on the whitework trade we must extrapolate from knowledge of practices in related trades, such as that of workers in precious threads, to determine how work might have been carried out and distributed in the 18th century. Even here we have difficulties: we must look to France and Diderot's Encyclopedia for one of the few accounts of the embroidery trade in the 18th century. Under the entry for 'BRODEUR' there is an illustration, reproduced in Plate I.2, of the interior of an embroidery workshop where work in precious threads was carried out. The scene includes two embroidery frames, of a general type with which we are still familiar today, on which fabric has been stretched for working; one frame is held upright to show the design for a waistcoat front marked out for embroidering while the other, on which an embroideress is working, is supported next to the window to make the most of natural daylight. Although only one woman is shown working at the frame, it is big enough to accommodate at least two, one on each side, and it was by no means uncommon for work to be shared and expedited in this way.

We can assume that whitework embroidery on this scale would likewise have been carried out in workshops with adequate room for large frames. Smaller frames were,

however, available for home use and can be seen in various 18th century portraits of ladies who were sufficiently proud of their accomplishments with the needle to be depicted at their work. Many professionals no doubt had to make do with simpler, cheaper versions but, for much whitework embroidery, it was essential for the fabric to be kept taut, with the warp and weft threads strictly at right angles to each other, as the work often involved thread-counting to achieve regular patterns.

In the later 18th century, a circular frame was introduced. This was known as a tambour frame from the French 'tambour' for drum because of its drum-like appearance when supporting the stretched fabric. Such frames were used particularly for working the new hooked chain stitch called tambouring after the frame. When this was taken up professionally in Scotland in the late 18th century, manufacturers equipped workshops with large rectangular frames with rollers at each end to carry whole webs of muslin. These were needed for the latest fashions in neo-classical dress that required millions of yards of embroidered muslin but more will be said of this work below.

Plate I.2 Detail from a page of Diderot's Encyclopedia, first published in 1751, showing an embroidery workshop.
The embroidery frame on the left would have been placed horizontally for the embroidery to be carried out with one end on a trestle and the other on the board secured beneath the window near the one already placed there. (Courtesy of Bristol University Library)

An alternative method of stretching fabric, which was particularly suitable for the fine, semi-transparent muslins used in much whitework, was simply to attach the fabric to a stiff supporting medium, such as parchment, card or even paper, carrying the design. The latter was sufficiently visible through the fabric for it to be worked and meant that the embroidery was readily portable, enabling ladies to carry work with them for mornings of congenial companionship with their friends or professionals to carry out the work within the confined space of a cottage or outside in good daylight, likewise often in company with other workers. Whatever the means used to stretch the fabric, the first requirement for any embroidery is a design.

Plate I.3 Detail from a page of a later supplement to Diderot's Encyclopedia showing a tambour frame. (Courtesy of Bristol University Library)

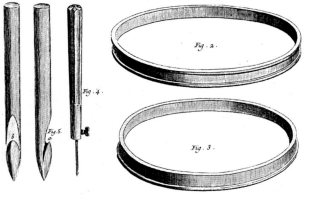

The design

In the 18th century, designs might be drawn by trained designers in the bigger professional workshops, by art teachers for ladies and their entourages or by the amateur embroideress herself, with all levels of skill in between. Books of patterns specifically for lace and embroideries had been available from the late 16th century and ladies continued to draw on these long after their initial publication but they also drew inspiration from the ever-increasing variety of books and prints available on natural history and other themes. Depictions of flowers had progressed through early herbals to 17th century Dutch still-life paintings and prints of massed flowers until the 18th century saw books of flower arrangements aimed specifically at workers in the decorative arts, including embroiderers: one famous early example was Robert Furber's 'The Flower Garden Displayed' first printed in 1732. Also available were wallpapers, patterned textiles, friends' embroideries and many other sources, all of which provided both amateur and professional with motifs for assimilation into a pleasing design. The final result depended on the aesthetic taste and abilities of the designer but, in general, accorded with fashions of the time: how these designs changed through the 18th century and how they related to other decorative arts of the period will be the subject of a later chapter.

Once drawn up and scaled to the correct proportions for an item to be embroidered, a design had to be transferred to the fabric to be worked. The first step usually involved the tracing of the designer's master copy onto a transparent medium such as oiled paper. The lines on the copy were then pricked through at close intervals and the copy firmly attached either to the fabric to be worked or, for transparent fabrics, to a card or other medium. A powder, or pounce, such as charcoal for light-coloured fabrics, was then dusted through the pricked holes to form lines of dots on the fabric or card and, once the pricking was removed, the dots could be joined to mark in the complete pattern and the whole process repeated, if necessary, to form pattern repeats. For semi-transparent fabrics, a quicker method was simply to trace the design directly onto the fabric while commercial production in late 18th century Ayrshire required a quicker method still and patterns were printed on the fabric in washable ink. Surprisingly, Charles Germain de Saint-Aubin, designer to Louis XV of France, in his 1770 treatise 'Art of the Embroiderer' states that, although black or blue ink would normally be used on light-coloured fabrics, a white preparation was preferable for white-on-white embroidery, especially on satin, as any white marks not covered by the embroidery would not harm the work. Whether this truly applied to muslin embroideries is not clear as Saint-Aubin's work is concerned more with embroidery in silk and metal threads than with cottons and linens.

Plate I.4 (right) Page from 'The Lady's Magazine' of 1785 showing 'A New Pattern for Sprigs'. 'The Lady's Magazine' was published from 1770 and often contained embroidery patterns for use by the purchaser. The pattern could have been traced or pricked and pounced to transfer the pattern to a fabric for working but some surviving patterns have pricked holes that do not fall on the lines in the design: a transparent fabric has been tacked directly on to them for working.

Plate I.5 (below) Detail from a two-inch deep (5cm) muslin border with an embroidery design marked in blue ink but unworked and of a similar border with the work started. The border includes numerous pattern repeats, involving numerous transfers of the original design: this task was quickened when printing was introduced.

Starting the embroidery

Before work could commence, the fabric had to be stretched, as outlined above, either on a frame or on a support marked with the design to be worked. Great care needed to be taken at this stage to ensure that warp and weft threads were kept strictly at right angles to each other, especially if the work were to involve any counted-thread embroidery.

The embroidery could now be started, but where? Unfinished examples demonstrate that people worked in different ways. Plate I.6, for example, shows a detail from a sleeve ruffle in which all the outlines of a design have been worked and the embroideress has just started filling in the leaves with close stitching. Plates I.8 and I.9, on the other hand, show details of the partly worked length in Plate I.5: in Plate I.8 areas of filling stitches have been worked but the outlines, in chain stitch, have just been started. In Plate I.9 the fillings and chain-stitch outlines are almost complete, the edge has been partly finished with buttonhole stitch and the fabric has been cut away adjacent the buttonhole stitches to leave a neat edge. A further unfinished work in the Exeter Museums collections also shows a pattern with only some fillings worked while a Danish sampler illustrated in 'Danish Pulled Thread Embroidery' by Fangel, Winckler & Madsen shows a pattern with the outlines completed before the fillings, as is the case in Plate I.7.

Plate I.6 (above) Detail from an unfinished sleeve ruffle. There is no sign of a design drawn on the fine muslin so presumably the fabric was tacked on to a pattern for working: the muslin is sufficiently transparent for a drawing to be seen through it. The outlines are worked in single running stitch, the stems in double running stitch; running stitch, or darning, is also used to fill in the leaves and petals.

Plate I.7 (right) Detail from a sleeve ruffle which is finished apart from the area of the border on the left which has not had its filling worked. Although this shows an alternative order of working, here the lack of fillings may be an oversight.

Plate I.8 (above) *Detail of the partly-worked embroidery in Plate I.5: areas of drawn-thread work have been completed but the chain-stitch outline has just been started at the left-hand end.*

Plate I.9 (right) *Detail of a different part of the embroidery in Plate I.5: the embroidery is almost complete and the embroideress has buttonholed part of the edge and cut away the excess fabric.*

Plate I.10 Unfinished border of appliqué work. A finer fabric is tacked over a denser fabric and threads have been couched down over most of the outlines of the design – some uncovered lines are seen on the right. On the left-hand side the backing fabric has been cut away where not wanted leaving dense areas of the pattern set off against semi-transparent ground: further details of appliqué work are shown in Plates I.11, I.11a.

Treatment of different areas of 18th century designs

In studying 18th-century embroideries, it is helpful to distinguish various features of the designs and to identify how these were worked. A limited number of stitches was used repeatedly for these features although those used on semi-transparent materials differed somewhat from those used on opaque fabrics or fine fabrics that were backed in use, for example, for making up into waistcoats and stomachers. The following résumé applies particularly to semi-transparent fabrics.

The most common stitches/techniques

(terms are explained below)

Lines (outlines and free lines): running stitch; couched threads (in early-mid 18th-century work); chain stitch (worked with a needle until about the 1760s but thereafter either with a needle or a tambour hook, the latter becoming more common); whipped running stitch (used more in the later 18th century); stem stitch (surprisingly little used); back stitch (used more often in opaque work).

Dense areas: applied second layer of fabric (in early-mid 18th-century work); shadow work; buttonholed satin stitch; satin stitch (more common on opaque fabrics and on transparent fabrics from the late 18th century onwards, particularly in the padded form); darning; whipped running stitch; tamboured chain stitch (from the 1760s).

Ground, or background: plain fabric; drawn-thread work.

Free edge: selvedge; raw edge rolled and/or strengthened by blanket, buttonhole or chain stitches; inverted blanket stitch leaving tufts of fabric like picots between stitches; added needle-worked loops or picots or bobbin picot edgings.

Other stitches: counted-thread fillings including drawn-thread work; eyelets kept open in various ways; seeding (used more often in opaque work).

GLOSSARY OF EMBROIDERY STITCHES AND TERMS

Appliqué work

Work in which a cord, fabric or other artefact is sewn on to the surface of a fabric: overcasting stitches are usually used over cords or to hold the cut edges of applied fabrics.

Plate I.11 (top right) Right side of appliqué work showing couched threads outlining denser pattern areas, comprising two layers of fabric, contrasted with the ground comprising a single layer. Overcast eyelets are also seen together with ladder stitch.
Plate I.11a (bottom right) Wrong side of appliqué work which is almost flat.

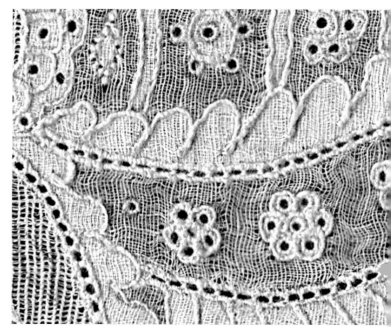

Back stitch

A stitch forming a continuous line of short stitches on one side, normally the right side, of a fabric and a row of longer, overlapping stitches on the other.

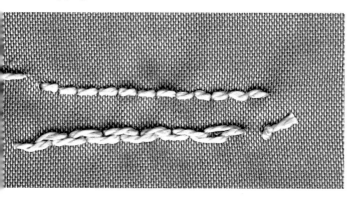

Plate I.12 (above) Back stitch; the right side (above) and the wrong side (below).

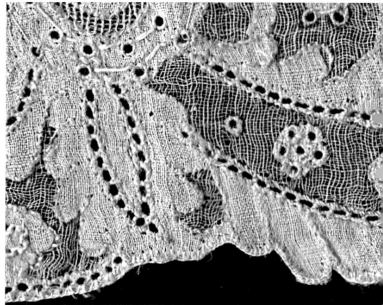

Blanket stitch and related stitches

Blanket stitch (basic) An L-shaped stitch with a base and upright of equal length at right angles to each other: the bases form a continuous line. In variations of this stitch the bases and uprights may be of different lengths and at an angle other than 90° to each other.

Buttonhole stitch (closely worked blanket stitch) I am following the practice of many embroidery and lace books in using this term for blanket stitch worked with the uprights so close together that they touch although this is not the true buttonhole stitch *(see 'Tailor's or true buttonhole stitch' below)*.

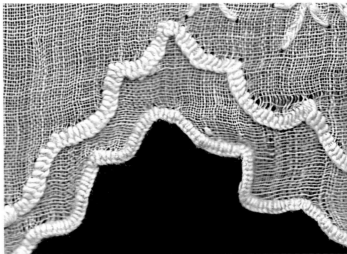

Plate I.14 (above) Edge neatened with a row of buttonhole stitches with a second row inside the edge.

Buttonholed wheel Blanket stitches worked with the bases forming a circle and the uprights extending towards the centre like the spokes of a wheel: the stitches are usually pulled tight to form a hole, or eyelet, in the centre.

Buttonholed eyelet Blanket stitches worked as in a buttonholed wheel but with the uprights touching. The central hole, or eyelet, may be pulled or cut (see Plate I.23).

Plate I.15 (below) Edge neatened with a row of buttonholed loops.

Plate I.13 (above) Detail of the sampler in Plate II.42 showing basic blanket stitch used as an outline down the centre and an inclined form at bottom centre; this is sometimes called 'single feather stitch'. Counted-thread, including drawn-thread fillings, and darning are also seen.

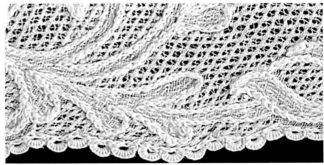

Inverted blanket stitch *(my term)* Blanket stitch worked along an edge but with the bases of the stitches forming a line inside the edge and the uprights extending over it. The uprights are often pulled tight so that a tuft of fabric protrudes between adjacent stitches; to the naked eye the tufts look like the picots of bobbin (Plate I.26) or needle lace.

Buttonholed satin stitch *(my term taken from the German term 'Plattslingstich' for this form of buttonhole stitch)* Buttonhole stitches worked so as to cover an area in a design like satin stitch but with one very distinct edge. This looks like satin stitch on the wrong side.

Tailor's or true buttonhole stitch Buttonhole stitch worked with an extra twist.

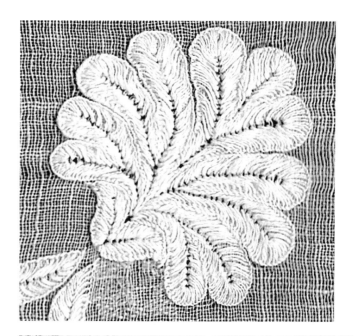

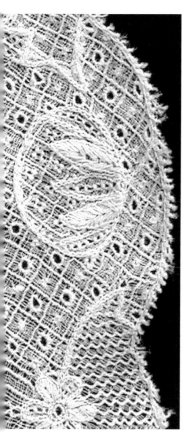

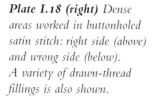

Plate I.16 (left) Edge with inverted blanket stitch producing tufts of fabric simulating picots: also many overcast eyelets.

Plate I.17 (above right) Motif worked in buttonholed satin stitch.

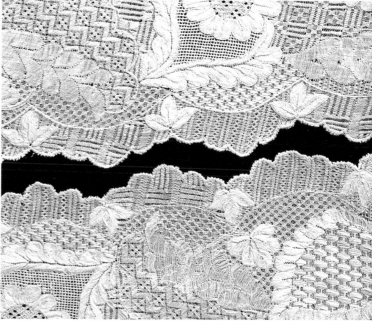

Plate I.18 (right) Dense areas worked in buttonholed satin stitch: right side (above) and wrong side (below). A variety of drawn-thread fillings is also shown.

Chain stitch A looped stitch worked in lines so as to look like a chain: it may be worked with **a needle or with a tambour hook**, the results being almost identical on the right side of the work. When worked with a tambour hook, a continuous line of straight stitches is formed on the reverse with thread running in and out of the same hole at each stitch: work with a needle produces less regular results, usually with two holes formed per stitch, and there are differences at the start and finish of work not visible here.★

*Plate I.19 (above left) Detail of an embroidery with lines worked in **chain stitch** with a needle.*

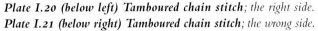

*Plate I.20 (below left) **Tamboured chain stitch**; the right side.*
*Plate I.21 (below right) **Tamboured chain stitch**; the wrong side.*

★ For an excellent exposition of the differences between needle-worked and tamboured chain stitch, see Gail Marsh's '*18th Century Embroidery Techniques*', Guild of Master Craftsmen Publications Ltd., 2006.

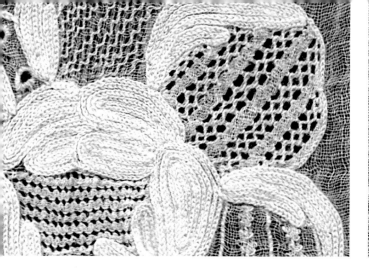

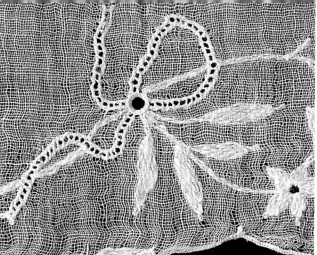

Plate I.22 (above) Tamboured chain stitch forming a dense area of pattern: fillings are in drawn-thread work.

Plate I.23 (above) Ladder stitch with a buttonholed eyelet (centre) and eyelet opened by darning (right).

Couching - *see 'Overcasting'*

Counted thread work Work in which stitches are placed extremely accurately by the counting of threads between positions in which a needle is inserted in a woven fabric: used to create areas of decorative geometric patterning – *see also 'Drawn-thread work' and Pulled-thread work.*

Darning - *see 'Running stitches'*

Double running – *see 'Running stitches'*

Drawn-thread work A form of counted-thread work in which embroidery threads are used to draw the fabric threads apart and so create decorative openwork patterns of holes and stitching. (Plates I.18, I.22) Also known as **pulled work** but in this book the term 'pulled work' is used for a different technique.

Eyelet A small round hole sometimes made for the passage of a cord but also purely for decoration. It may be kept open by various stitches: *see Buttonholed wheel, Buttonholed eyelet, Overcast eyelet.* (Plates I.11, I.16, I.23).

Filling/Filling Stitch A fancy stitch used for decorative effect to fill a space in lace or embroidery. There are numerous such stitches, many involving counted-thread work.

Ladder stitch Two parallel overcast lines with overcast threads crossing between them forming a row of rectangular holes, the whole looking like a ladder. There are more complex versions of this basic stitch.

Needle-weaving A technique in which a thread is worked in and out and back and forth through a set of parallel threads or the meshes of a net to create an area resembling woven fabric.

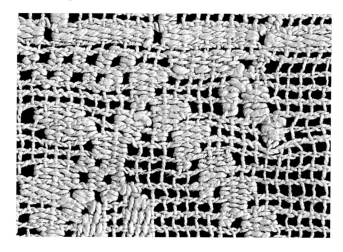

Plate I.24 (above) A woven, square-meshed net decorated with needle-weaving.

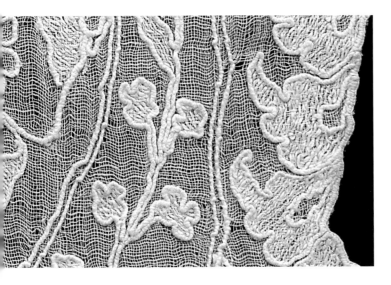

Openwork embroidery Term for various embroidery techniques in which holes are formed in a fabric.

Overcasting A sewing technique in which a series of stitches is worked along a line but with each stitch at an angle to the line: used to hold a rolled edge in place, to prevent a cut edge from fraying or to hold a thread or cord laid on a surface in which case it is called **'couching'** (Plates I.11, I.25).

Overcast eyelet An eyelet in which the hole is kept open by overcasting: the hole may be cut but is more often formed by a stiletto (Plate I.11).

Oversewing A term sometimes used instead of 'overcasting' but more properly used for similar but much closer stitching used to seam two edges together.

Padded satin stitch - *see 'Satin stitches'*.

Picot A small projecting loop or point usually formed to decorate an edge.

Plate I.25 (above) Overcasting used to attach a thread to a fabric; the right side. Dense pattern areas are created by darning.

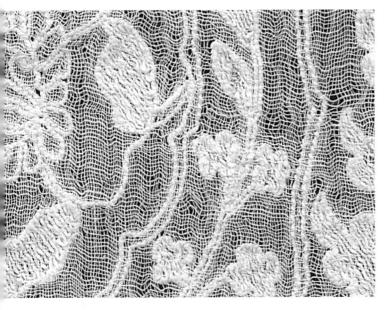

Plate I.25a (above) Overcasting; the wrong side.

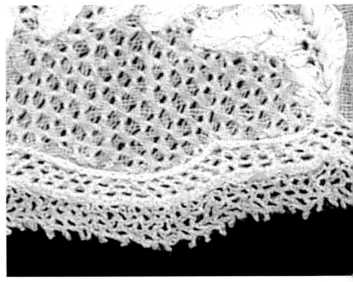

Plate I.26 (above) An edge finished with a sewn-on bobbin-made border with picots: a wide variety of such borders was used.

Pulled-thread work (Plates I.30, I.30a) A form of counted-thread work in which some threads are cut and pulled out of the fabric to leave open areas crossed by other threads which are pulled together, strengthened and decorated by embroidery threads: also known as **drawn-thread work** or, more properly, **drawn-fabric work** but, in this book, the term 'drawn-thread work' is used for a different technique. The cutting and removal of threads weakens the fabric: pulled-thread work is not common in fine 18th-century embroidery.

Running stitches
Basic (or single) A line of stitches worked in and out of the fabric creating alternating stitches and spaces on both the right and wrong sides. (Plate I.27): in decorative work stitches on the right side are often longer for greater effect.
Darning Lines of running stitches worked back and forth closely side by side: the basic use of this technique is to strengthen or mend a weak area of fabric but, in embroideries, it is used to create a dense area of pattern (Plates I.13, I.27).
Double running – two lines of running stitches side by side, usually worked in opposite directions (Plate I.27).

Plate I.27 Single running stitch outlines dense areas created by darning while double running forms the stems; eyelets are kept open by the stitching.

Plate I.28 (A 19th century embroidery; the right side)
All single lines are in whipped running stitch; motifs are in padded satin stitch except the diamonds which are in shadow work. The edge is neatened with scallops of buttonhole stitch.

Whipped running Running stitches in which, once a line has been run, the thread is worked, or whipped, back through the stitches on the surface with an overcasting stitch: the overcasting thread should not penetrate the fabric but often does: often combined with other stitches to form dense pattern areas (Plate I.28).

Plate I.28a The wrong side of the embroidery in Plate I.28.

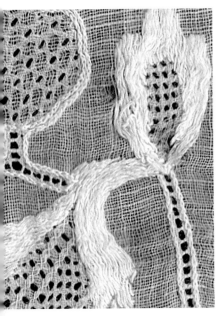

Plate I.29 (top left) *Dense areas are worked in a combination of long running stitches and whipped running stitch; the ladder stitch has chain stitch along each side.*

Plate I.29a (bottom left) *The wrong side of the embroidery in Plate I.29: fewer stitches show as the whipping on the right side should not penetrate the fabric – in practice, some stitches often do.*

Plate I.30 (top right) *(A 19th century embroidery; the right side) Dense areas are worked in satin stitch and lines are in stem stitch: in 18th century work the stitches are usually shorter and closer together. The openwork is pulled-thread work: threads are cut and removed to create openings.*

Satin stitches
Basic Satin stitch
Straight stitches worked closely side by side across a design motif or area so as to cover it completely and form a smooth, satin-like surface (Plate I.30).
Padded satin stitch
Satin stitch worked over padding usually formed by previously worked stitches filling the area to be covered: the result is a smooth, raised surface (Plate I.28).

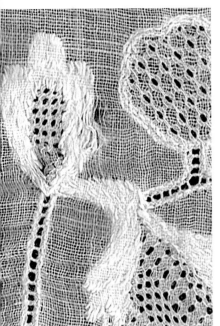

Plate I.30a (above) *The wrong side of the embroidery in Plate I.30.*

Plate I.31 (left) Embroidery with dense areas in shiny satin stitch, couched-cord outlines and seeding in the flower to the left.

Plate I.32 (top right) Shadow work: the right side. Stems are double rows of chain stitch.
Plate I.32a (bottom right) Shadow work; the wrong side.

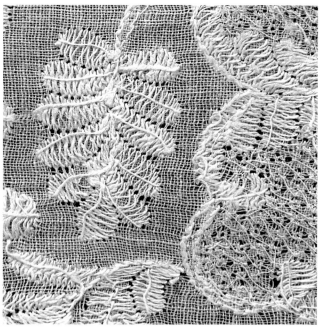

Seed stitch/Seeding A scatter of embroidered dots used as a decorative filling. The dots may be made by: running stitches, usually with shorter stitches on the right side than on the reverse; back stitches; or knotted stitches.

Shadow work Embroidery on the wrong side of a semi-transparent fabric that is seen as an opaque area on the right side: usually created by herringbone stitch on the wrong side that is seen as a continuous line of minute stitches, like back stitches, around the opaque area on the right side.

Stem stitch A line of stitches worked at a slight angle to the line with each stitch starting halfway along the previous stitch. (Plate I.28)

Stiletto holes Holes, or eyelets, made by forcing a stiletto (a pointed tool) through a fabric.

Tambour work/ Tambouring –
see 'Chain stitch'.

Whipping A term most properly used for a technique in which an edge is loosely overcast and then the sewing thread is drawn up to gather the fabric but commonly used as an alternative to overcasting – *see 'Whipped running'.*

Whitework/whitework embroidery Any embroidery in white thread on a white fabric.

18TH CENTURY WHITE ACCESSORIES IN CONTEXT

MAIN FORMS OF WOMEN'S DRESS THROUGH THE 18TH CENTURY

Having considered the basic embroidery and how it was carried out, we can now look at its use on costume accessories in the 18th century but, first, a brief look at the dress itself. Throughout our period women of all classes wore a long-skirted robe, or gown, over at least one waist-length petticoat, with a chemise, or shift, of linen or cotton next to the skin. The gown was normally front-opening until the very end of the century and worn over stays, which supported and shaped the torso, and additional under petticoats and/or stiffened frames or padding which gave a fashionable line to the skirt.

The skirt might be open at the front to disclose a dress petticoat or closed in the form known as a 'round gown'. The front edges of the bodice might also meet and be pinned or otherwise fastened together in wear but often they defined a V-shaped gap filled either by the stays, if these were covered in a rich fabric, or more usually by a separate, decorative stomacher. The neckline was usually low but partly filled by a frill called a tucker: this was often but not always attached around the neckline of the chemise and might be made of the same material or of finer fabric: lace is often shown in portraits. A separate frill, or modesty piece, might also stand up from the front edge of the neckline.

For much of the century the bodice sleeves ended just above or below the elbow and, in the first half of the period, were cut fairly wide so that the sleeves of the shift showed beneath them: the 18th-century attitude to underwear was not the same as our own. For working women the sleeves would be finished with a simple band but wealthier classes would often display their status by one or more added ruffles that fell elegantly behind the elbow.

The actual structure of the robe changed through the century, with various types being in use contemporaneously, often for different occasions, but such changes need not concern us here. What is more relevant is the gradual change in line and aesthetics which affected the shape and style of accessories worn with the dress. The following sketches, though illustrating specific forms of dress, are given to show the general changes that occurred through the century.

A mantua; 1700-10
The early line was slim and vertical compared with later decades. The mantua's trained skirt is looped back over the hips to disclose a decorative petticoat. The chemise sleeves, with their added ruffles, show beneath the wide, loose sleeves of the bodice. A tucker softens the neckline and a frilled cap is worn on the head.

An English fitted round gown; mid 1730s

The term 'round gown' signifies that the robe skirt is closed, covering the petticoat: the shape is softly rounded but the bodice is long and drops to a point below the waistline. A muslin handkerchief, or kerchief, round the neck is tucked under lacing over the stomacher.

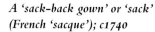

A 'sack-back gown' or 'sack' (French 'sacque'); c1740

The box pleats at the back, which hang freely to the floor, distinguish this form of gown, developed in France but worn in England from about the 1720s, from the English gown with its fitted back. Beneath the loose pleats, the bodice is fitted over the stays: a hooped petticoat or frame gives the skirt its distended shape.

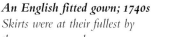

An English fitted gown; 1740s

Skirts were at their fullest by the 1740s-50s and might be domed, as here, fan-shaped (flattened at the front) or project directly out from the hips so as to present a broad rectangle to the viewer. The overall appearance was severe, with minimal decoration.

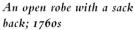

An open robe with a sack back; 1760s

By the 1760s the sack was worn for formal occasions but was decorated in a similar manner to informal robes, if more ostentatiously. Ruched and gathered trimmings of the dress fabric were common.

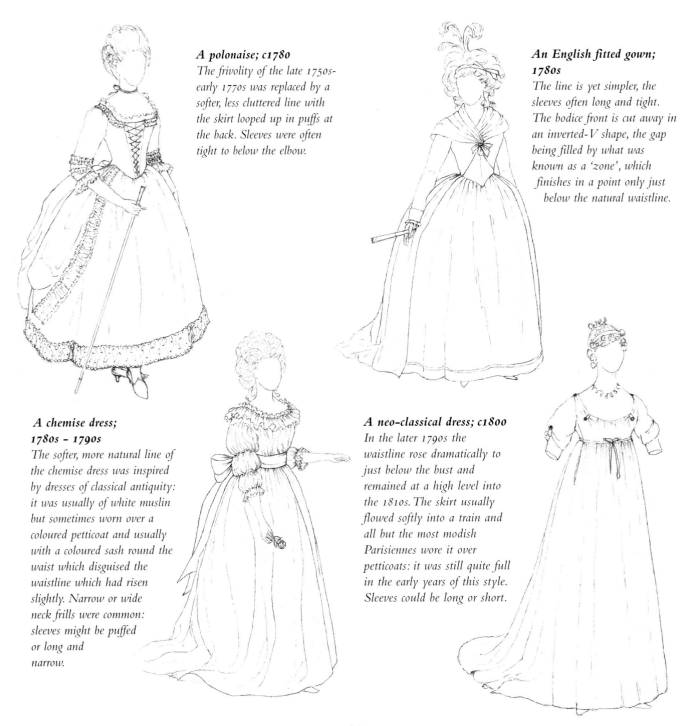

A polonaise; c1780

The frivolity of the late 1750s-early 1770s was replaced by a softer, less cluttered line with the skirt looped up in puffs at the back. Sleeves were often tight to below the elbow.

An English fitted gown; 1780s

The line is yet simpler, the sleeves often long and tight. The bodice front is cut away in an inverted-V shape, the gap being filled by what was known as a 'zone', which finishes in a point only just below the natural waistline.

A chemise dress; 1780s - 1790s

The softer, more natural line of the chemise dress was inspired by dresses of classical antiquity: it was usually of white muslin but sometimes worn over a coloured petticoat and usually with a coloured sash round the waist which disguised the waistline which had risen slightly. Narrow or wide neck frills were common: sleeves might be puffed or long and narrow.

A neo-classical dress; c1800

In the later 1790s the waistline rose dramatically to just below the bust and remained at a high level into the 1810s. The skirt usually flowed softly into a train and all but the most modish Parisiennes wore it over petticoats: it was still quite full in the early years of this style. Sleeves could be long or short.

WHITE ACCESSORIES: CHANGING SHAPES AND MODES OF WEAR

Plate II.1 *Detail from a portrait of Mr. and Mrs. Bull and family, c1740-42 (Photograph reproduced by kind permission of the Harris Museum and Art Gallery)*
Mrs. Bull, in the centre, wears an open robe of silk satin over a petticoat which is visible beneath the diaphanous apron.
A kerchief round her shoulders is tucked under a single ribbon tie across her bosom while her robe sleeves are finished with cuffs of the dress fabric with ruffles of fine lawn or muslin falling beneath them.
The older lady's kerchief is tucked under ties, or stays, which lace the front edges of her bodice together; the latter are faced with flat robings of the patterned dress fabric. The young girl holds her apron, in which she has a mass of flowers, in her left hand: her cuffs and white ruffles are less full than her mother's and her neckline is trimmed with a narrow frill called a tucker.
All three females wear caps, the women's having lappets that are tied under the chin: these informal caps are of a different form from the formal cap seen in Plate II.7.

The father and son also have white ruffles at the wrists: these are attached to the wrist bands finishing the shirt sleeves; the son also has a neck frill while his father wears a cravat with the ends tucked into the top of his waistcoat.

Plate II.2 *Half-handkerchief,*
or kerchief, of embroidered
muslin; c1750-75.
This shows the triangular form
of kerchief: a square cut on the
diagonal. The embroidery is of
the type known as 'Dresden
work' and, from its high quality
and careful arrangement and
variety of the drawn-thread
fillings, may well have been
made in Saxony. The large,
stylised flowers in its design
almost match the scale of those
in the earlier dress fabric with
which the kerchief is shown in
Plate II.2b but the playful
nature of the ribbon coiling
through it suggests a later date:
more will be said on this aspect
of the embroidery below.

Although the structures of the main garments just described differed from each other and changed through the century, their main lines varied more or less in unison, as did many subsidiary features and the accessories worn with them. As we have seen, almost throughout the period, the neckline was low, whether rounded, as was usual in a closed-bodied gown, or square. The décolletage was partly disguised by the tucker and sometimes an additional modesty frill but these provided little warmth and it was customary for ladies to wear some sort of covering around the shoulders. According to the literature, such coverings could take many forms, from scarves and tippets to hooded capes and shawls, and might be made from any of a variety of materials from silk taffetas, gauzes and lace to warmer fabrics but what are depicted most often are white handkerchiefs, often with a lace edging. Inventories and other records most often describe these as made from 'cambric' or 'Holland', both forms of fine linen, or 'calico' or 'muslin', both cottons, but surviving examples which concern us, which are decorated with white embroidery, are most usually of muslin. It is not always clear from portraits whether the handkerchiefs shown are complete squares, folded on the diagonal and worn with the folded corners brought down the front of the bodice, or are triangles cut from a square and worn in a similar manner; surviving examples show that both forms were in use, as were triangles with the neck edge scooped out into a curve (Plate II.4). All might have been called 'handkerchiefs' at the time although the terms 'neckerchief' and 'kerchief', with variations in spelling, were also in general use, as was the term 'half-handkerchief' for the triangular form: the term 'pocket handkerchief' was generally used for what we would now call a handkerchief.

In the early decades of the century, for which there are relatively few portraits, handkerchiefs are shown draped loosely around the neckline but the 1730s-40s brought a change in style to a more severe look. Bodices were shaped into stiff cones over the stays and the only decorations were

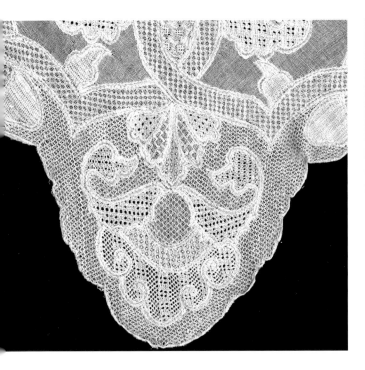

flat robings of the dress fabric extending down the front edges to end below the natural waistline.

The main fabrics of the period were also stiff and of relatively heavy weight: letters and inventories speak of a wide variety of substantial cotton, woollen, linen and mixed-fibre fabrics while portraits most often show dense, lustrous silk satins in sombre hues. Handkerchiefs could contribute to the severity of this image: many portraits, such as that of the Bull family in Plate II.1, show them carefully folded and tucked neatly inside the stays or under ribbons or cords crossing the stomacher at the front.

Sleeves varied in width and length but, in general, were fairly loosely cut and finished just above or below the elbow in cuffs of the dress material, sometimes, in the 1740s, extended into stiffened wings behind. Cotton or linen sleeve ruffles were still worn as in previous decades but tended to be less full and flowing. These sleeve ruffles were also accessories as, although attached to the chemise in wear, they were made

Plate II.2a (top left) *Detail of the kerchief in Plate II.2 The design outlines are worked in chain stitch: the border is completely filled with drawn-thread work which forms a ground for the motifs, while different drawn-thread stitches form the fillings.*

Plate II.2b (above) *The kerchief in Plate II.2 shown over a robe from the Devonshire Collection of Period Costume, Totnes. The robe is made from a silk brocade of about the 1730s but has been altered for later wear. It was not just the front necklines of robes that were low-cut: kerchiefs also protected the back of the neck while the beauty of the design is also best seen from the back.*

Plate II.3 (left) A mid-18th century sleeve ruffle decorated with whitework embroidery; the fine ruffle is gathered onto a tape which would have been sewn to the band finishing the end of the chemise sleeve. Fine ruffles, such as this, would have been removed for laundering as they were very expensive and needed special care; they then had to be reattached. In wear the wide part of the ruffle was allowed to fall behind the elbow.

The decoration is in fine Dresden work; the right (outermost) side of the work is distinguished by a fine applied cord forming lines in the design but both sides are beautifully finished.

Plate II.3a (below) Detail of the ruffle in Plate II.3 showing the applied cord, shadow work and drawn-thread fillings.

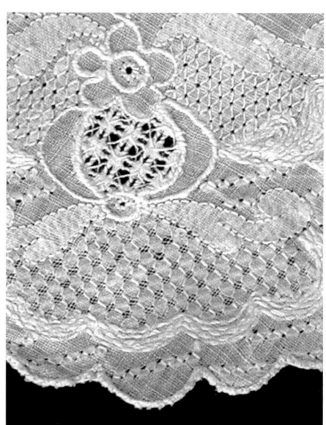

separately and gathered to the bands finishing the sleeve ends. Many were especially shaped to have a wider portion which fell behind the elbow and a narrower portion in front, the seam joining the two ends into a circle being carefully arranged in line with the hidden sleeve seam so as to fall in the least conspicuous position in wear.

For informal wear, like the tucker, ruffles might be of plain linen or cotton fabric, perhaps of the same material as the shift, but often they were of a finer lawn or muslin and even informal portraits, such as were fashionable in the 18th century, show the use of fine lace. More formal portraits also show tiers of lace trimming surrounding the sleeves themselves but, if such trimmings were ever made in whitework, they have not survived or are no longer recognisable as such, and do not fall within the scope of this work.

Unfortunately few portraits show the use of embroidered muslin accessories, the main theme of this work, but it is clear from inventories and other documents that, like lace, they were often made in sets, or suits, including matching ruffles, a kerchief and/or apron and possibly other accessories such as a cap and trimmings. Portraits also show that men wore decorative ruffles at the wrists and down the fronts of their shirts but the only evidence that these were made in whitework rather than plain fabrics or lace is again documentary as I have seen no surviving examples and very few illustrations.

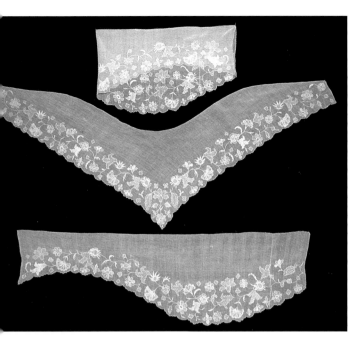

Plate II.4 (above) *A matching set of muslin sleeve ruffles and kerchief decorated with whitework embroidery; c1760-80. Although such sets were common in the 18th century, few have survived. The lower ruffle shows the typical shaping of late 18th century ruffles: these have a straight edge for gathering to a band and the opposite edge cut into an S-shaped curve. The curve tends to be more marked in later examples than in ruffles of the 1730s-40s: patterns for both styles are shown on pages 155 and 163.*
The ruffles are slightly unusual in being cut from more than one width of fabric. The ends, which are of equal depth, are formed by the selvedges and can be joined by oversewing to form almost invisible seams but the shaping is such that the seams would fall in the least conspicuous positions. The upper ruffle is shown folded ready for the seam to be sewn before gathering to a band.
The kerchief in this set has a scooped neckline and straight-cut ends: it is more usual for kerchiefs to taper to the corners.

Plate II.4a (right) *Detail of the ruffle in Plate II.4 showing the wealth of fillings and beautifully buttonholed, scalloped edge.*

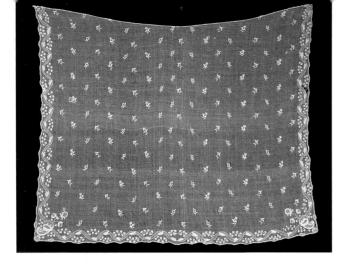

Plate II.5 (above) Late 18th century apron of typical size and shape. The apron would be gathered or pleated onto a waistband for wear. The dip in the top edge, though slight, is deliberate and follows the line of the top edge of skirts and petticoats of the period: it accommodates the usual V-shape of the bodice or stomacher in wear (see Plates II.10, II.13). W - 44in (112cm); Ls - 35in (89cm); Lc - 33in (84cm).

Plate II.5a Detail of the apron in Plate II.5: the main stitches are tamboured chain stitch and drawn-thread work.

The third major white accessory in everyday use was the apron. Nowadays we associate aprons with working life but it is clear from portraits, letters and other records of the period that, in Britain, provided they were of appropriately expensive fabric, they were acceptable wear on all but the most formal occasions. One recalls the incident in which Beau Nash, Master of Ceremonies at the Bath assembly rooms, tore a lace apron off the Duchess of Queensbury saying 'Only Abigails wear aprons', meaning that aprons were part of servants' dress (Abigail being a lower-class name) and absolutely unacceptable for a formal ball, yet the Duchess was sufficiently proud of her apron to want to wear it on such a public occasion.

An apron made of lace, a hand-made artefact, more expensive than the finest woven silks, was, however, exceptional. In most portraiture what we see is the long, plain white apron, sometimes edged with lace, which reaches, or almost reaches, the hemline of the robe or petticoat and which dips beneath the pointed waistline of the bodice: most surviving white aprons are, indeed, of that order of length and have a shallow V-shaped dip at the waistband and it is largely these that concern us.

There are few portraits that show us how such aprons were worn at the beginning of the century but there are numerous ones from the 1730s onwards. By this time the skirt, which had been relatively narrow and bunched at the back, had widened and, in the 1740s −1750s, reached its greatest extremes.

One might expect that aprons would likewise have been narrower in the earlier period, would have widened as skirts expanded and would have collapsed thereafter and, indeed, the earliest aprons studied, from the 1710s-20s, are somewhat narrower, of the order of one yard (90cm) wide: most later ones tend to be about 50in (125cm) wide but there is no clear evolution. Most surviving aprons are cut from a single width of material, usually muslin, sometimes linen. There are occasional exceptions, those made from one and a half or two widths of fabric, but their designs do not link them definitively to the middle decades of the century. Nor do portraits show wider ones in the middle period: on the contrary, many dresses from the 1730s to 1750s are adorned with aprons that occupy a narrow vertical field of the skirt or petticoat whereas a greater expanse of the skirt may be covered in later decades.

Although portraiture most usually depicts long white aprons and these certainly survive in substantial numbers in British collections, another common, though rarely depicted survival from the early to middle years of the 18th century, is a short silk type lavishly decorated with fine silk and/or metal-thread embroidery. These aprons would have been far more expensive than muslin aprons and were worn on more formal occasions. An unusual white example of this type is shown in Plate II.6.

While considering formal dress, another accessory that concerns us is the formal cap with decorative lappets that came into being at the very end of the 17th century and was used throughout the 18th century. Many were made from the finest laces but a few examples can be found in whitework from the early to mid 18th century. Their construction was simple: a roughly semi-circular piece of lace formed the cap back or crown and was partly surrounded by a narrow, gathered frill which, in wear, framed the face.

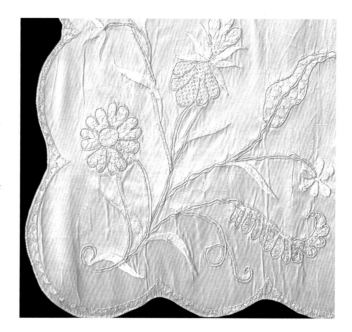

Plate II.6a (above) Detail of the apron in Plate II.6.

Plate II.6 (right) Short apron in ivory-coloured silk with self-coloured embroidery. Short silk aprons were worn for more formal occasions than muslin or lawn aprons and were particularly popular with the wide skirts of the 1730s-50s. Many extremely elaborate examples survive in costume collections although they are rarely shown in portraits. They would have been very expensive and were stored away carefully when not in use. This example is much simpler than the norm: the embroidery is amateur work.

The lappets, or streamers, were attached to the back and could be allowed to hang freely, tied under the chin or pinned up on top as etiquette or taste demanded. Such caps are rarely seen in portraits which more usually feature informal headwear, an area not investigated due to its complexity, but are important survivals as the lace examples show the changing tastes in design to perfection.

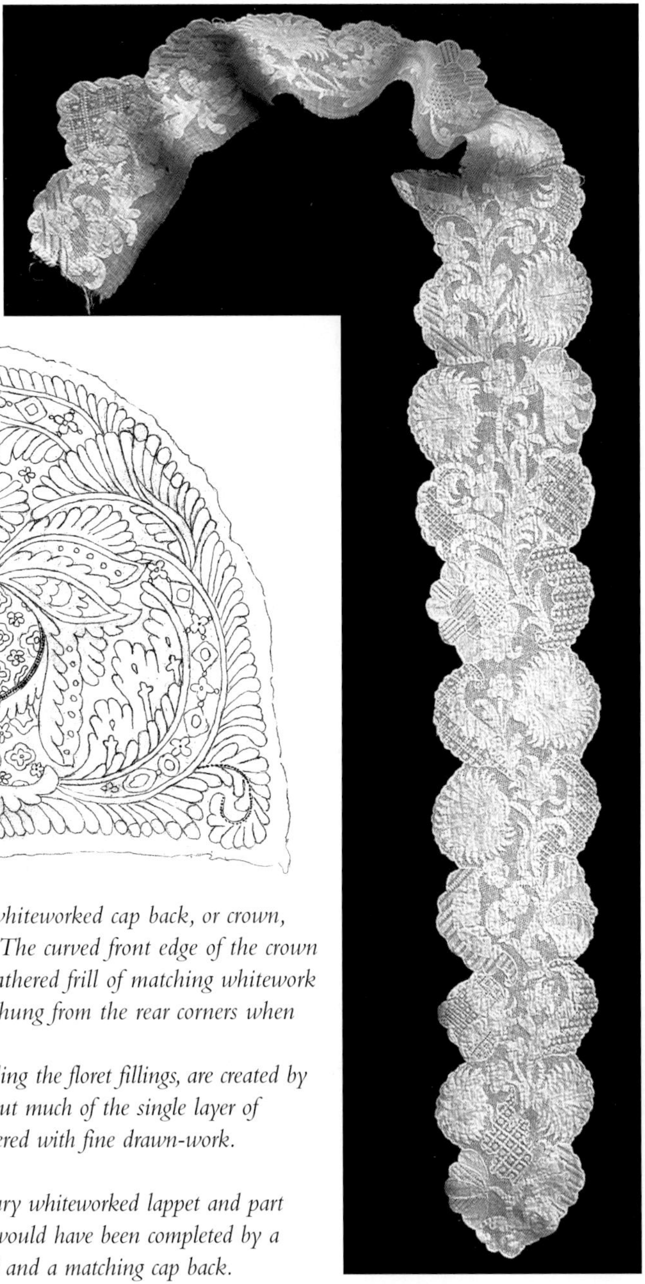

Plate II.7 (below) A court mantua of the mid-1730s worn with a formal headdress comprising a cap with lappets.

Plate II.8 (above) Drawing of a whiteworked cap back, or crown, from the V&A collection; c1725-50. The curved front edge of the crown would have been trimmed with a gathered frill of matching whitework while a pair of lappets would have hung from the rear corners when the cap was completed.

The dense areas of the design, including the floret fillings, are created by appliqué work with corded outlines but much of the single layer of muslin around the motifs is embroidered with fine drawn-work.

Plate II.9 (right) A mid-18th century whiteworked lappet and part of the frill for a formal cap. The cap would have been completed by a second lappet, a further length of frill and a matching cap back.

After the middle of the century superficial changes in women's dress came more quickly. Ridiculously wide skirts were no longer worn except for court occasions and the whole appearance of dress was softened by a change in fabrics and trimmings: heavy satins gave way to lighter-weight silks in gayer colours and the bodice robings, which had been severe and plain, were often ruched and/or edged with decorative braid or snaked down the bodice front and on down the skirt.

From about 1755 the stiff sleeve cuffs were also replaced by one or more shaped frills of the dress material arranged to fall behind the elbow. White muslin, lawn or lace ruffles were still worn beneath these frills and, according to portraiture, were particularly wide in the 1760s, with double or triple ruffles becoming far more common. As the robe sleeves tightened in the 1750s, it became more usual for the flowing white ruffles to be sewn inside the ends of the robe sleeves themselves rather than to the chemise.

From this time on, engravings showing contemporary fashions became far more widespread and, along with portraits, give a fuller picture of how dress evolved generally to the end of the century and of the variations appropriate to different types of occasion. A few examples must suffice to show how aprons, kerchiefs and sleeve ruffles also changed to meet the changing demands of the times.

1758.

Plate II.10 *Print showing a 'Lady in the dress of 1758' (Courtesy of Hereford Museum and Art Gallery)*
The lady's yellow open robe, worn over a contrasting blue petticoat, is far more elaborately decorated than those of earlier decades. Most importantly for our subject, the bodice sleeves are finished with double falling cuffs or frills of the dress material which are pinked to match the edges of the skirt and beneath which are flowing triple white ruffles with van-Dycked edges (cut into points).
A short cape or kerchief around the neckline has been coloured blue but could equally well have been white. The white apron, gathered beneath the waistline, falls short of the petticoat hemline so as not to hide a line of applied decoration around the bottom, a style that was to become more common in the 1760s-70s.
The details of the all-over, scrolling, floral design of the apron unfortunately cannot be distinguished. Aprons with such elaborate borders as this are not common in collections.
The lady also carries a white pocket handkerchief in her hand.

1764

Plate II.12 (left) *Print of 1764 showing a lady, seated, being shown some goods by a maid or trader: from a scrap book in the Hereford Museum and Art Gallery collection. The lady's kerchief is thrown loosely round her neck and draped down the bodice which is open to reveal a striped stomacher. She also wears a full-length apron and white sleeve ruffles. The maid also wears a kerchief, here in black and tucked into her bodice which is closed down the front. Her chemise sleeves end in simple bands rather than ruffles and her robe still has the older style of cuff. She appears to be wearing an apron hitched up to one side but the colouring confuses this part of the picture.*

Plate II.11 (above) *Triple sleeve ruffle, c1760-80: Accession No.PH184, Pickford House Derby.*
The three layers of the ruffle are graduated in size with the narrowest one uppermost. All three layers are gathered and attached to a single tape which, at this date, would probably be sewn inside the end of the robe sleeve for wear rather than to the chemise. The rococo trailing stem design is in chain stitch; drawn-thread work fills in the large border motifs. The edges are softened with a minute bobbin trimming with picots.

Plate II.11a (above) *View of the triple sleeve ruffle in Plate II.11 from above.*

Plate II.13 (right) *Portrait of Dorothy Quincy, wife of John Hancock, one of the signatories of the American Declaration of Independence and Governor of Massachusetts: by John Singleton Copley, (American, 1738-1815), c1772. (Oil on canvas, 50 1/8in x 39 5/8in - 127.32cm x 100.65cm; Museum of Fine Arts, Boston, USA; Charles H. Bayley Picture and Painting Fund and Gift of Mrs. Ann B. Loring, 1975.13) Photograph © 2008 Museum of Fine Arts, Boston, USA.*

Dorothy's pink silk robe has a matching stomacher decorated with a large ribbon bow at the neckline which is softened by a white tucker, probably of lace. Her diaphanous apron is of muslin embroidered with large floral sprays: similar examples will be seen in Plates

II.56-II.59. The bodice has falling cuffs of the dress material worn with triple sleeve ruffles probably of whiteworked muslin rather than lace. A narrow inner ruffle can also be seen around Dorothy's right elbow: this may be attached to the chemise sleeve whereas the triple ruffle would most likely have been sewn inside the end of the robe sleeve. Few such narrow ruffles survive but they can sometimes be seen in portraits where the arm is held at a suitable angle.

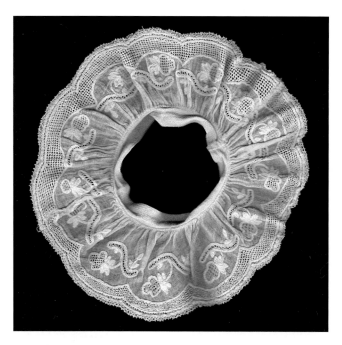

1778.

Plate II.14 *Narrow sleeve ruffle of whiteworked muslin gathered to a linen band. A narrow ruffle like this might have been worn beneath wider ruffles as seen in the portrait of Dorothy Quincy (Plate II.13). Alternatively it might have been worn on its own, particularly with the new sleeve shaping of the later 1770s, or with long sleeves (Plate II.16). This ruffle is made from a simple length of embroidered fabric, not shaped like previously-seen ruffles, but single ruffles with slight shaping were also worn with the new fashion, as seen in Plate II.15.*
The muslin has a slightly scalloped edge trimmed with a narrow bobbin lace with picots. Inside this are a band of drawn-thread work and discrete strawberry-like motifs carried on ladder-stitched stems.

Plate II.15 (above right) *Print showing two dresses of 1778 (courtesy of the Hereford Museum and Art Gallery).*
The skirt of the lady on the right is looped up at the back in soft folds in the style known as 'à la polonaise'. Both ladies wear aprons which are not so long as to cover the decoration on their petticoats which are shortened to show the ankle. The aprons also appear to be much wider than in earlier images, each extending to cover the sides

of the skirt rather than just the central field. Both ladies also wear full kerchiefs folded on the diagonal and hanging loosely at the back but with the ends tucked into the edges of the bodice at the front. The lady on the right also appears to have a second, smaller kerchief knotted round her neck. The lady on the right has elbow-length sleeves with an overlay of the dress fabric and single, small white sleeve ruffles. The lady on the left has longer, tight sleeves, also with narrow ruffles. The ladies' hairstyles, topped by their magnificent hats, are much higher and fuller than in previous decades.

The more relaxed mood of the third quarter of the century appears to have brought little change in the shape and use of kerchiefs; they continued to be tucked in at times although are perhaps more often seen draped loosely around the neck and allowed to fall negligently down the front of the bodice. Lace capes, particularly hooded capes, were also more prevalent as an alternative.

By the mid 1770s, the skirt was being bunched or puffed in the style known as the 'polonaise' and it became more common for the petticoat, visible beneath the skirt of the robe, to be trimmed with ruched flounces of the dress fabric or other lightweight trimming. A shorter version of the white apron might be worn over this (one example has been seen in Plate II.10: two more are shown in Plate II.15) but full-length aprons also continued to be worn throughout this period.

As the skirts changed in the 1770s, so did the sleeves. These were now lengthened to just below the elbow and their falls of dress fabric were often replaced by an overlay of pleated or gathered material, sometimes but not always the same as the dress.

This new style was not so suited to wide falling ruffles and these were often discarded in favour of simple, narrow frills which might or might not be shaped; one frill that might have been used with this style is shown in Plate II.14. This was not an entirely new fashion: long-sleeved gowns with such frills were sometimes worn earlier in the century and became much more common in the 1780s-90s but, as with all fashions, not everyone gave up the earlier styles so that falling ruffles survived into the 1790s.

By the 1780s, more radical changes were in the air. The neo-classical style, which had already taken hold in other decorative arts and portraiture, now affected everyday dress: the elaborate layers of decoration of previous decades were discarded in favour of simple, flowing lines. Skirts remained full at the back and sides but were again allowed to fall gracefully to the ground and even lighter fabrics, particularly muslins, became popular. Despite these changes, aprons and kerchiefs continued to be worn. It even became fashionable to wear a kerchief over the head instead of a cap but, more particularly, kerchiefs started to become more voluminous.

Virtue preserved by Deception.

Plate II.16 *Illustration, probably from a pocket book of the early 1780s, entitled 'Virtue preserved by Deception'.*
Although not designed specifically as fashion plates, such illustrations often show dress of their period. Here the lady not only wears a voluminous kerchief around her shoulders but also carries a long shawl or stole draped over her arm. Her robe still has a very full skirt but it is uncluttered by any form of decoration and has been lengthened into a train at the back. It has long, tight sleeves. The hairstyle has widened and is topped by an even broader-brimmed hat than in the 1770s.

1786.

Plate II.17 (right) Fashion illustration from a scrap album in the Hampshire Museums collections showing dress of 1791. There is little change in the dress since the 1780s but this plate shows an alternative way of wearing a kerchief with the ends crossed over at the front and tied or otherwise fastened at the back. The skirt, which would probably have been made from printed muslin, has a deep but simple repetitive pattern right round the hemline. The kerchief also has a repetitive border pattern of floral sprigs.
Such patterns might have been printed or embroidered: similar patterns are well represented in whitework collections.

Plate II.18 (above) Fashion illustration from a scrap album in the Hampshire Museums collections showing hats, hairstyles and handkerchiefs of 1786. The wide, frizzed dressing of the hair, wide-brimmed hats and large handkerchiefs, or buffons, puffed up over the breasts are typical of styles in the 1780s.

By the middle of the decade they were being puffed up under the chin in a form termed a 'buffon' giving an appearance that has been likened to that of a pouter pigeon. Large or long handkerchiefs might alternatively be worn with their ends crossed over at the front and tied or pinned at the back. Many kerchiefs are also depicted with a gathered frill around the edge but, despite their ubiquity in portraiture and fashion plates, I have seen few surviving examples.

1791.

Plate II.19 Detail from a fashion illustration of 1789 from a scrap album in the Hereford Museum and Art Gallery collections. The lady on the right wears a buffon with a pleated frill around the edge and a circular pleated collar close around her neck: this may well be a separate accessory. The lady on the left has a circular pleated collar around her neckline and a kerchief or shawl around her shoulders. The collar is probably attached to her dress.

Plate II.20 Fashion illustration from a scrap album in the Hampshire Museums collections showing dress of 1797. The waistline of the lady's dress is now high under her bust. She wears a kerchief over her head instead of a cap but an extremely wide variety of headwear was worn at this time.

Through the 1790s skirts narrowed and, towards the end of the decade, the waistline rose dramatically bringing in the neo-classical look with which we are familiar. As white muslin was fashionable for the dress itself, white accessories were no longer so desirable. Nevertheless, kerchiefs continued to be worn into the 19th century and there were also white versions of what we might now call a stole. These developed from the long shawls that were imported from Kashmir in the late 18th century and were all the rage by the early 19th century: their elongate shape suited the fashion for flowing drapery and, at the time, might have been called handkerchiefs, shawls or any one of a variety of innovative names according to details of shape and trimming. The only other change in our three major accessories at this time was in the aprons. The narrow line of the robe could not accommodate the wide aprons of previous decades and their place was occasionally taken by narrower ones but the paucity of surviving examples suggests that they were no longer so popular.

Naturally, even in a century when change was much slower than in our own, the fashion scene in the 18th century was far more complex than indicated by this brief résumé but it is now time to look at the embroidery, the main theme of this work.

PROMENADE DRESSES *1799.*

Plate II.21 (above left) *Fashion illustration showing 'Promenade dresses' of 1799.*

The slimmer skirt lines and high waists of these ladies' dresses make them look dramatically different from those in earlier decades although the skirts are still fuller than they were to become. They are worn with long, flowing accessories which accentuate the new look: that on the left is a simple rectangular long shawl in transparent muslin whereas that on the right is a more complex wrap with sleeves and gathered frills decorated with a tiny repeat sprig design. The hair is dressed much closer to the head again and hats have shrunk commensurately.

Plate II.22 (below) *Apron; 1790s-early 1800s.*

This is not only narrower than earlier aprons, in line with the slim skirt line of the period, it is also shorter. The fabric is partly pleated onto a waistband which ends in short loops; in this period robe skirts often had draw strings which tied round the waist and these would have been passed through the apron loops to fasten it round the waist at the same time. The embroidery is mainly in satin stitch and very coarse drawn-thread work with lines of knots. The edge is buttonhole stitch, probably worked over an applied thread.

W - 36.75in (93.5cm); Lc − 31in (79cm)+1.75in (4.5cm) into scallop. The top edge is pleated into the waistband at the sides (7.25 + 6.75in) but the centre(3.25in) is plain; total length of band − 21in (53.5cm) including open loops 1.75in (4.5cm) each.

CHANGING WHITEWORK DESIGNS ON ACCESSORIES IN SEMI-TRANSPARENT FABRICS

The early 18th century

Although this book deals primarily with 18th-century whitework, it is helpful to look briefly at what went before. By the early 17th century, bleached linen thread, which has a white to off-white colour, had been used in European clothing for thousands of years, both in plain-woven and more decorative forms, while cotton was starting to become more common. White embroideries, many in openwork techniques, were used by the wealthy for costume and household purposes alongside bobbin and needle laces which were by then exceeding them in extravagance.

By the 1660s the techniques of lace-making had developed to such a degree that one of the most prestigious of all laces, if not all textiles, emerged: this was Venetian rose point, a three-dimensional luxury sought by all the aristocracy of Europe but, as with all such luxuries, not everyone could afford the real article. Now was the time for embroidery, the precursor of needle lace, to provide a cheaper alternative. Pattern motifs, imitating the baroque original, were cut from woven fabric, linked by needle-made bars and embellished with raised surface work created either as in the original or, more cheaply, by the application of pre-made cords around outlines in the design.

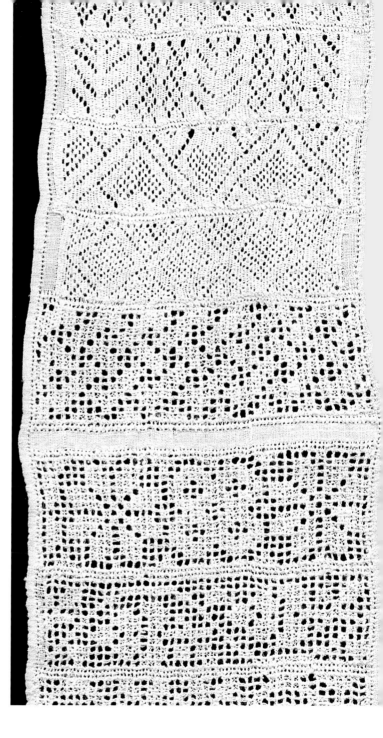

Plate II.23 Detail from a late-17th- century whiteworked sampler showing a wide variety of pulled- and drawn-thread stitches, mostly in purely geometric patterns. This is only one of the many whitework crafts that were popular in the 17th century: plain surface embroidery, cutwork, bobbin- and needle-lace making and embroidery on woven and knotted nets are just some of the others. All were carried out both professionally and by amateurs particularly to embellish articles that needed regular washing.
W – 4.75in (12cm).

Plate II.24 (left) Late 17th century Venetian raised needlepoint, or 'rose point'. The bold baroque design of scrolling exotic flowers and leaves is typical of the mid-second half of the 17th century. Laces such as this were worked entirely with a needle and thread in stitches based on the buttonhole stitch: areas of more open stitching, or fillings, contrast with denser areas of the motifs. Cutwork embroidery copies were also available: in these the motifs, which are cut from woven fabric, are decorated with arrays of eyelets and drawn- or pulled-thread work imitating the filling stitches of the original. Applied cords are often used as substitutes for the graduated raised work seen here which is worked over a padding of linen threads. D – 3.8in (9.5cm).

By the end of the century, bold patterns were out of vogue and the designs of costume lace had degenerated to a mass of tiny motifs, some still organised in scrolling patterns, some based on axes of symmetry in the new French manner, others in totally random formations. The lack of obvious design did not matter when lace was gathered to create a frivolous, frothy effect but this was desired only for formal occasions. By 1700 the Flemish linen industry was able to produce ultra-fine woven fabrics that were a joy in their own right while more and more fine cottons were being imported from India and the Middle East. These, without any embellishment, were used for sleeve ruffles, caps and lappets and any other trimmings where white lace might previously have been used.

Although lace was out of fashion in dress, patterned fabrics and embroideries were still popular for both costume and household furnishings. Indian printed chintzes (cotton fabrics with exotic designs and usually a glazed surface) and crewel works (embroidery in wool usually on a linen base), which had been fashionable for much of the 17th century, were still in vogue and it is from these sources that designs

Plate II.25 (below) Venetian flat needlepoint with an irregular pattern of tiny motifs; c1700. D – 4.8in (12.5cm).

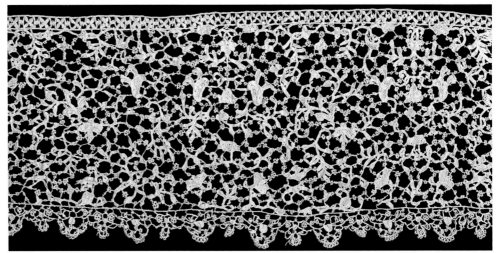

for our earliest 18th century whiteworked accessories appear to have been drawn.

Fortunately for us there was a vogue for signing and dating work in the first quarter of the 18th century as several dated whiteworked aprons or panels survive from this period. One of the earliest is illustrated in 'Needlework through the ages' by Symmonds and Preece: it is worked with a 'tree-of-life' design with the date and initials '1709-18 MH' (for Mary Holden) in the mound on which the tree stands. Another apron with an extremely similar design, clearly taken from the same source, is illustrated in Plate II.27. This is in the V&A collections and bears the text '1717 14th year of her age Mary Tyrrell' along with various religious texts in the mounds of pattern repeats of the design. Two other similar aprons or panels in the collections are worked with '1718 IR' and '1713 Mary Greene ' (Plate II.26) although, confusingly, this latter also bears the name 'Mary March 1745' and other initials. Although, in general, one would take the latest date on a piece of work to be the actual date of working, the stylistic similarity between the dated examples mentioned suggests that, in this case, the later date is a subsequent addition, perhaps worked by the original embroideress in later life or by her descendant.

Plate II.26 (above) *Drawing of a pattern repeat from a muslin apron; Accession No. T 164-1975, V&A. The pattern on this apron is a 'tree-of-life' design which is repeated in each quadrant of the apron. The mound of each repeat is worked with a different name or initials; this repeat bears the text '1713 Mary Greene'.*

The 'tree-of-life' design was extremely popular in large-scale furnishing fabrics, such as bedspreads and hangings, from the 17th century through into the early 18th century. Here it is worked in white thread, mainly in darning, or running, stitch on semi-transparent muslin. Typically, the long, curving, pointed, stylised leaves and/or petals are combined to form large motifs which spring from rather spindly branches. Some leaves and flower centres are enlivened with filling stitches which, like the text, are worked by needle-weaving on a drawn-thread ground.

W – 34in (86.5cm) (selvedge at right; 3/8in (0.5cm) hem at left);
Ls – 36in (91.5cm).

1717 Mary Tyrell
in the 14th year of her age

V + A Apron
1564 - 1909

CF

Plate II.27 *Drawing of part of a muslin apron; Accession No. 1564-1904, V&A.*

The design of this apron is again based on the tree of life but only the pattern repeat in the lower central portion of the apron shown is complete; those to the left, right and in the upper portion are incomplete. Each mound contains a different text: that shown reads 'REMEMBER NOW THY CREATOR IN THE'; another reads '1717 14th year of her age Mary Tyrrell'.

The outsize, exotic birds with their raised wings and long tail feathers appear in many examples of this design. Although the basic design is old, the arch-like shape of the trunk and lowest branch of this design, the marked asymmetry, the scattering of motifs drawn to different scales and the geometric patterning within the motifs themselves are all features of the so-called 'bizarre' silks of the 1700s-1710s, discussed below. This apron is worked on a complete fabric width; W - 32in (81.3cm): Lc - 30in (76cm); Ls - 32in (81.3cm).

Plate II.28 *Detail of a panel worked in a similar manner to the aprons in Plates II.26 and II.28. The dense areas are darned while the open net filling is drawn-thread work.*

All of the aprons and panels in this group are worked in fairly simple stitching: the sinuous branches which form the primary structure of the designs are in running, or darning, stitch, worked in close, parallel lines, creating densely patterned areas which contrast with the transparent muslin ground. The same stitch is also used for many of the leaves, flowers and exotic birds which frequently flutter amongst them. A few areas may be decorated with openwork fillings but these are mostly worked in a different manner from the later type of drawn filling with which we are generally familiar. Some are simply a regular open grid, or net, of drawn-work: in others the embroideress has first created the grid and then patterned it either with geometric designs or with letters of the worker's name or other text. Needle-weaving is most often used for the patterning although satin stitch is an alternative: all these techniques would have been part of a girl's repertoire of needlework in the late 17th to early 18th centuries.

Plate II.29 (right) Panel with four repeats of a pattern based on the
'tree of life' but with more delicate treatment of the motif than in the
V&A examples. The top edges of the two upper repeats are unfinished
leaving a narrow band of plain muslin which has clearly been stitched
in the past: one assumes it has been gathered to a waist band for wear.
In addition to the main design, this panel is unusual in having narrow
border designs down each side: each comprises two rows of discrete
motifs arranged at 90° to the orientation of the tree-of-life motifs.
These small motifs include simple floral sprays, birds and very strange
combinations of buildings and vegetation (see Plate II.29a) which may
be derived from early 18th century 'bizarre' designs although the light
treatment of the main design suggests a slightly later date.

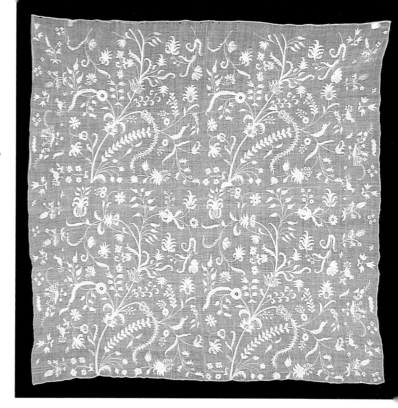

Plate II.29a Detail of the
panel in Plate II.29 showing a
curious motif including what
appear to be buildings standing
on a mound with flowers and
foliage.
See p46 for further detail.

45

The 'tree-of-life' design is often used on a large scale, covering a substantial area, but, in most of the whiteworked panels illustrated, which are of the order of a yard (1 metre) square, about four pattern repeats are used to fill the article. In some cases these are neatly arranged to fill the four quadrants of the panel (Plate II.29) but, more often, the repeats are broken at top and bottom and/or at the sides even though these consist of the selvedges of the fabric. It would appear that the original intention of the designer was for the fabric to be worked in long lengths for cutting and sewing to make much larger articles: this would have been a common practice for professional embroiderers but, surprisingly, some of the dated works, which one assumes are amateur pieces and which have been made up into aprons, are designed in this manner.

The latest dated design of this type that I have seen is on a superb apron in the Nottingham Museum collection: this is initialled and dated E.W.1721 (Plate II.30). Here the trees retain the spindly form of the earlier embroideries and are worked in the same manner but the major floral motifs are much more substantial, the birds much more exotic and all provide space for a profusion of filling stitches. Even the mounds on which the trees stand are more like clouds than hillocks and, in addition to the large flowers, some of which are recognisably European, the branches sprout a multitude of curling tendrils carrying tiny flower heads that fill the spaces between the more major motifs.

Plate II.29b Detail of the panel in Plate II.29 showing various embroidery stitches including chain stitch, herringbone stitch, darning, stem stitch and drawn-thread work.

1720/1 SOUTH SEA BUBBLE COLLAPSE
1721 WEARING OF ENGLISH PRINTED COTTONS MADE ILLEGAL
1721-1742 SIR ROBERT WALPOLE LEADS GOVERNMENT
1726 'GULLIVER'S TRAVELS' BY DEAN SWIFT
1727 GEORGE II SUCCEEDS
1728 'BEGGARS' OPERA' BY GAY

Plate II.30 *Muslin apron initialled and dated 'E.W.1721' in a flower near the top left-hand corner; Accession No.1976-117, Museum of Costume and Textiles, Nottingham. The basic pattern on this apron consists of a tree carrying two birds, one above the other. This is repeated almost six times, three repeats horizontally and two vertically, but the repeats are not identical. Some features, such as the rose at top centre, are not repeated at all and filling stitches vary enormously from one repeat to the next: some are worked in two stages like those on the earlier aprons but others are worked in a single process as in the Dresden work which we shall see below. The very playful nature of this design shows the influence that the rococo style was having on textiles by the 1720s.*
W – 35in (89cm);
Lc – 30in (76cm).

Plate II.31 *Portrait of unknown Lady by George Beare; c1740-50 (©Roy Miles Fine Paintings/ Bridgeman Art Library, BAL 17905).*

This lady is wearing a very expensive black robe with gold lace applied over the cuffs and down either side of her bodice opening. Her fine muslin kerchief, tucked under buckled stays connecting the edges of her bodice, is probably edged with lace rather than whitework. The matching double sleeve ruffles are clearly attached to her chemise sleeves seen under the decorated robe cuffs. Her apron, on the other hand, is decorated with discrete floral sprays in a variation of the tree-of-life design but with no obvious pattern repeat and no openwork fillings.

A clear white line divides the central panel from the border pattern which appears to be different from that on the kerchief and sleeve ruffles.

A similar design arrangement is seen on the apron in Plate II.32.

Although the lady's robe is in the style of about 1740, the apron could be earlier. It is clearly of high quality: is it an old favourite or a highly prized new purchase?

The Nottingham apron may have the latest dated tree-of-life design but similar aprons were still in use in the 1740s as evidenced by a portrait by George Beare from that decade (Plate II.31) and suggested by Mary Green's apron of 1713 which also bears the text 'Mary March 1745'. The apron in the Beare portrait is interesting in that its central panel, which contains large-scale floral designs, is surrounded by a very different border pattern. Although the scale of the central design is very similar to that of the tree-of-life designs, the flowers do not appear to spring from trees growing from mounds but are carried on very curvaceous stems: the resulting flower sprays are separate but placed very close together with no obvious repetition. The stylish and playful nature of the sprays is perhaps even more similar to that of the small floral sprays seen in the Valenciennes laces in Plate II.33 than to the tree-of-life design. The apron as a whole resembles another example in the V&A collection (Plate II.32), which has a central panel with four floral sprays surrounded by a separate border. The border is not only worked in a totally different manner from the central design but is in a different style, similar to that of other designs of the 1720s-40s which we shall see below.

Plate II.32 *Drawing of a corner of a Muslin apron; Accession No. T381-1967, V&A.*
This apron has a main panel with four full pattern repeats of a tree-of-life style design plus extra narrow portions of the pattern on the right-hand side. Most of the work is similar to that of previous aprons but some of the main stems are in an openwork technique. In addition, it has a border sewn to the main panel down the two sides and along the bottom, being gathered round the corners. The design of the added border is worked almost entirely in outline: there are a few geometric fillings but no drawn-thread work. One cannot tell whether the border was added when the apron was made originally or at a later date: its design would have been fashionable at any time in the second quarter of the 18th century.
W - 39in (99cm): Lc - 36in (91.5cm); Ls - 38.5in (98cm).

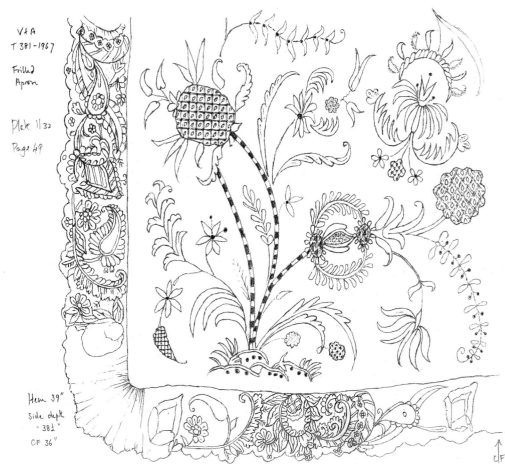

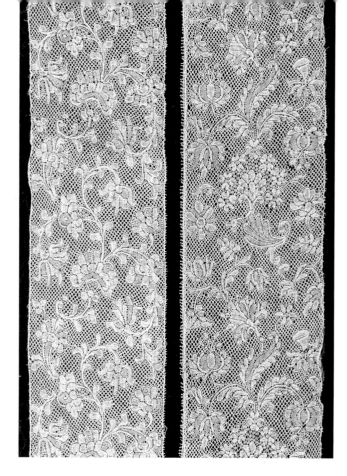

Plate II.33 *Two borders of early-18th century Valenciennes bobbin lace with designs of flower sprays based on C- and S-shaped scrolls. The motifs are worked in cloth stitch and the lighter half stitch against five-hole grounds. The asymmetry and lightness of character of the floral sprays are typically rococo: the sprays even spring from curved stems or shell-like motifs. Laces, like these, made in the finest Flemish linen thread of the period could rival even the gauze-like muslins imported from India and helped bring lace back into fashion. There is also a resemblance to the much larger sprays on the apron worn by the lady in Plate II.31.*
W – 2.8in(7.4 cm); Pr - 3in(7.6 cm): W – 3in (7.6 cm); Pr -5.4in (13.2cm).

★ *See Santina Levey,'Lace: a History' for an illustration.*

Before looking at other works from the1720s-40s, with their alternative styling, we shall return to the beginning of the century to see how they developed. At that time, as already seen in Plate II.25, lace designs had become minimalist and lace was somewhat out of fashion: there was a need for a new impetus in design. One style that had remained in use in woven fabrics from the late 17th century was a repetitive array of small, stylised floral sprays. In the early 18th century these were affected by the new rococo aesthetics: they were made more curvaceous and playful and were also taken up in lace designs, particularly in the extremely delicate Flemish laces of Valenciennes where they floated against a cobweb ground (Plate II.33). Not surprisingly, then, whitework embroideries also had their versions: a portrait of Mademoiselle de Béthisy and her brother★, painted by Belle in 1714 and now in the Musée de Versailles, shows the young girl wearing a muslin apron decorated all over with such sprays. The fine stems flow in S- or C-shaped curves from the very bottom and break into tiny leaves, flowerheads and scrolling tendrils, the lines being even more delicate than in their lace counterparts.

While some old ideas continued to be reused and reinvented, a totally new trend was also affecting the lace scene. In the late 17th century, startling exotic designs, now termed 'bizarre', had been introduced into French woven silks and had become highly fashionable. These were characterised by the juxtaposition of strange geometric shapes, exotic flowers, fruit and architectural motifs, all in utterly different relative proportions from real life: strong diagonal movement, asymmetry; and odd colour contrasts were also apparent while larger motifs or spaces were filled with geometric and floral patterns.

The influence of the architectural aspect of these designs has already been seen in Mary Tyrrell's whiteworked apron in Plate II.27 and the small border motifs of the panel in Plates II.29, 29a but the designs as a whole had an even more marked effect on the lace industry, particularly those from the late 1710s onwards. By this time the designs had become modified; motifs tended to be larger and more crowded, there was more emphasis on flowers, fruits and foliage, and ribbons of complex patterning often rippled through them. Also, despite the continued emphasis on movement, motifs were more often arranged around vertical axes of symmetry: an example of this style is seen in Plate II.34. The design here is extremely crowded and it is difficult to discern its various components but they include symmetrical palmette motifs in the centre.

As styles progressed through the 1710s into the 1720s, the palmettes became more significant and were set in clear spaces surrounded by mirror-imaged arrangements of flowers, foliage and geometric shapes, often intertwined with intricately patterned ribbons which snaked up and down the length of the silk. The geometric patterning filling the ribbons and other motifs give this style its current name of 'lace pattern' but it is not certain that it was derived from, rather than preceded, similar designs in laces.

Plates II.34 Panel of a 'bizarre' silk damask of about the 1720s from a dress made up at a later date (courtesy of the Hereford Museum and Art Gallery).
In this woven silk, two large leaf shapes enclosing smaller leaf shapes like a set of Russian dolls spread symmetrically from a floral base which supports a palmette design of scrolls and leaves surmounted by a patterned circle surrounded by flower-like geometric shapes. Two intertwined complex ribbons of patterning also spread symmetrically outwardly and upwardly to form a frame for the palmette and the floral base of the next pattern repeat above it. This is typical of the scale, complexity and density of silk designs of the late 1710s-early 1730s.

Lace designers, working in a single colour and in small areas, usually narrow bands, could not copy the silk designs exactly but adopted some features, particularly the rhythm and density of patterning. This can mean that designs are difficult to read except at close quarters but, coming after a period in which plain white fabrics were fashionable, it minimised the apparent differences between the materials. The style is best seen in the bobbin laces of Brussels (see plate 36), Mechlin and Valenciennes, particularly in the caps and lappets of the period, many made for the finest headdresses for court wear and therefore designed and worked to the highest standards. Lace was once more in fashion and it was again time for embroideresses to provide cheap imitations for the growing middle-class populations of Europe. A drawing of one example of a whiteworked cap back has already been seen in Plate II.8: another example from the V&A collection is shown in Plate II.35. This is a superb example of the bizarre style and must date from the late 1710s to early 1730s. Rather more whiteworked lappets survive than crowns though they are still not numerous. Several, though undated, display such a striking resemblance to their lace counterparts that they can also reasonably be attributed to about the same date or slightly later: it would be dangerous to assume that whitework is of identical date to related high-fashion silks or laces given the time it took for designs to spread beyond the fashionable community and for copies to be made. Various examples are shown in the following plates together with bobbin-lace lappets that they resemble.

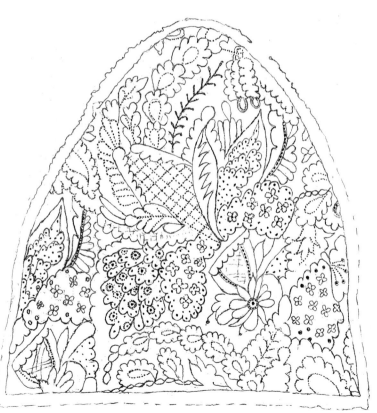

Plate II.35 *Drawing of an unfinished cap back, or crown, in appliqué work. V&A.*
The crown would have been made en suite with lappets and a frill and possibly other costume accessories. The ogival shape is fairly typical of early 18th century crowns: later crowns tend to be more rounded.
Dense areas of the pattern are created by two layers of fabric. Lines within these denser areas are formed by rows of eyelets while eyelets are also used as fillings. Most openwork areas are created by drawn-thread work but two small areas of fabric are cut away and the spaces filled with needlepoint lace stitches.
The complexity of the design, scale of motifs and use of filling stitches are comparable with those of the bizarre silk in Plate II.34: the complete asymmetry may be due to earlier bizarre designs in which patterning spread diagonally across the fabric, or to its derivation from one half of a silk 'lace' pattern, like that of the central Brussels lace lappet in Plate II.36. Lace crowns from the second quarter of the 18th century tend to have symmetrical designs suggesting that this crown design is derived directly from a woven fabric rather than via a lace.
The Temple Newsam Collection, Leeds, has a fairly similar crown.

Plate II.36 *Centre: Brussels bobbin lace lappet in a very dense 'bizarre' design of about 1715-25. As in the damask in Plate II.34 the design is very complex, with a strong sense of movement, but the narrow width of the lace cannot accommodate the full symmetrical design of the silk: instead the lace pattern is derived from half the silk pattern and swings from side to side up and down the length of the lappet.*

Left and right: two different whiteworked lappets imitating Brussels bobbin lace (the right-hand lappet is altered by the addition of a square of similar work at the top through which it is joined to the second lappet of the pair, not shown).

The right-hand lappet is worked in a much denser fabric than that on the left. Both lappets not only imitate the style of the central lappet but also have applied surface work imitating the raised work of Brussels bobbin laces – see Plates II.36a-c for details. The shape of these lappets, tapering to an almost square end, is typical of the 1710s-20s. Lappet lengths: left - 20in (51cm); centre - 24.5in (62cm); right (excluding square)- 20in (51cm).

53

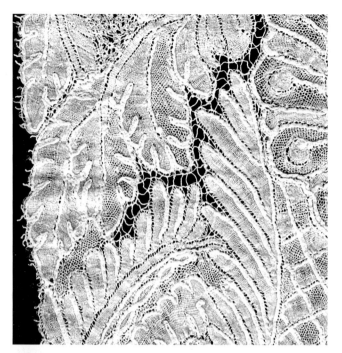

Plate II.36a (left) Detail of the Brussels lace in Plate II.36 showing the typical structure. Some areas resemble woven fabric but the threads vary direction, following contours in the design, unlike the threads in the embroidered copies in which the warps and wefts are parallel and perpendicular to the edges. Other areas are in more open structures while some features are emphasised by narrow bobbin-worked tapes on the surface. The bobbin-made picots on the edge are an integral part of the work.

Plate II.36b (below left) Detail of the right-hand lappet in Plate II.36. This is worked in a single thickness of fine but dense fabric. The design is worked in chain stitch and lines of a double overcasting stitch. The whole is lightened by overcast and buttonholed eyelets and the edge is buttonholed.

Plate II.36c (below right) Detail of the left-hand lappet in Plate II.36. This has much more complex work on a finer fabric than the right-hand lappet. Raised outlines are worked with a couched thread and what appears to be a couched braid. Open lines and fillings are in drawn-thread work. The picots are probably worked with the embroidery thread.

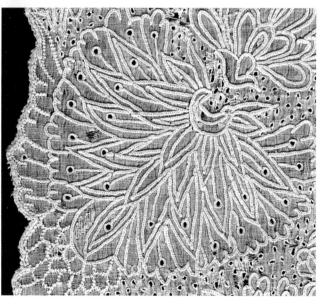

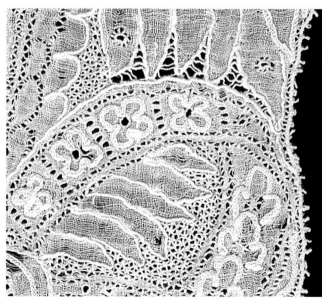

In wear the lappets shown in Plate II.36 would have been attached to a cap and worn in the manner shown on page 32. Accounts show that whiteworked lappets, like lace, were made and sold in sets with the cap back and frill for surrounding the face and sometimes also with other trimmings or accessories, such as sleeve ruffles, kerchiefs and/or aprons. Alas, I have come across no such sets: I know of only one lappet with part of its frill attached (Plate II.9) while, of the few cap backs found, two are in the V&A collections and are shown in Plates II.8 and II.35 while a third is in the Temple Newsam collection, Leeds. The Whittington Art Gallery, Manchester also holds three cap backs but these come from a German collection and do not necessarily fit into the British social scene.

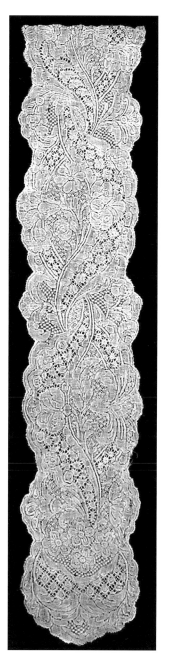
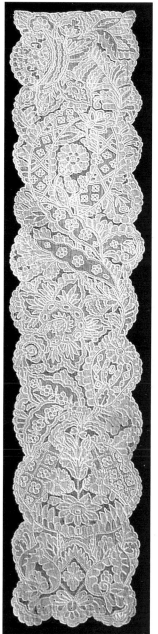

Plate II.37 (right) Valenciennes bobbin lace lappet in a 'lace-pattern' design; c late 1720s. This lappet, with its greater use of ribbons of complex patterning, is probably of slightly later date than the Brussels lappet in Plate II.36. In Valenciennes laces the floral motifs and ribbons are differentiated from the complex grounds and fillings only by narrow lines of openwork: there is no raised work. The separate flower heads in the ribbons are a common filling in all Flemish laces of this period. The rounded end of the lappet and unevenly scalloped edges are typical of the late 1720s-1740s. Symmetrical motifs are also common at the bottom of such lappets even though the rest of the design is asymmetric and sways from side to side.
W – 3.5in (9cm).

Plate II.38 (far right) A whiteworked lappet in a lace pattern similar to that of the lappet in Plate II.37; late 1720s-1730s. A second layer of applied muslin creates the dense areas of the design including the flower heads which, like those in the Valenciennes lappet, constitute fillings in the ribbons and other spaces in the design. The couched threads outlining the pattern and fillings make the pattern stand out more clearly than in the Valenciennes lappet: in this respect the lappet resembles a Brussels or Mechlin bobbin lace or a French needlepoint.
L – 21.5in (54.5cm); W – 4.5in (11.5cm).

Plate II.39 *Fabric scrap with a bizarre design of about the late 1720s - early 1730s. The design of this scrap has the same strong sense of movement as the silk in Plate II.34 but it is rather less complex and has greater naturalism.*

Plate II.40 *Pair of whiteworked lappets with a vigorous, undulating design worked in an appliqué technique; c1730s. The large fruit-like bodies near the top are very similar to the central fruit in Plate II.39.*

In the late 1720s, designs started to open out although motifs, if anything, became larger. A woven silk from about this period is shown in Plate II.39 with a pair of whiteworked lappets of similar design in Plate II.40. The edging of the apron in Plate II.32 has a similar, though more confused, design. Despite the number of lappets shown here, I have found very few additional examples during my research. Most of these are in the V&A and display a similar variety of whitework techniques to those illustrated. Clearly, in this period, embroideresses experimented by creating copies of laces in various ways and it is impossible to say with certainty whether surviving examples are amateur or professional work or whereabouts in Europe they were made. At the same time, however, a very particular form of whitework was developing that, although adopted throughout Europe, was to become associated with a specific area: this was 'Dresden work', also known as 'Dresden lace' or 'point de Saxe', from its major sources in Dresden and the surrounding area of Saxony in Eastern Germany.

Plate II.40a *Detail of a lappet in Plate II.40 showing the slight contrast between the denser areas of design created by two layers of fabric and the more transparent areas formed by a single layer. Couched threads both outline the appliqué work and form other lines in the design. Drawn-thread work and overcast eyelets are used for the fillings while the edge is finished with an applied thread held by buttonhole stitches and an added bobbin picot trimming. L – 21.5in (54.5cm); W – 4.6in (11.8cm)*

1733-5 Hogarth's print series 'The Rake's Progress'
1738 John Kay's flying shuttle uses one operative on a broad loom instead of two
1739 War of Jenkin's Ear over Atlantic trade control; Thomas Coram founds the Foundling Hospital
1740 'Pamela' by S. Richardson

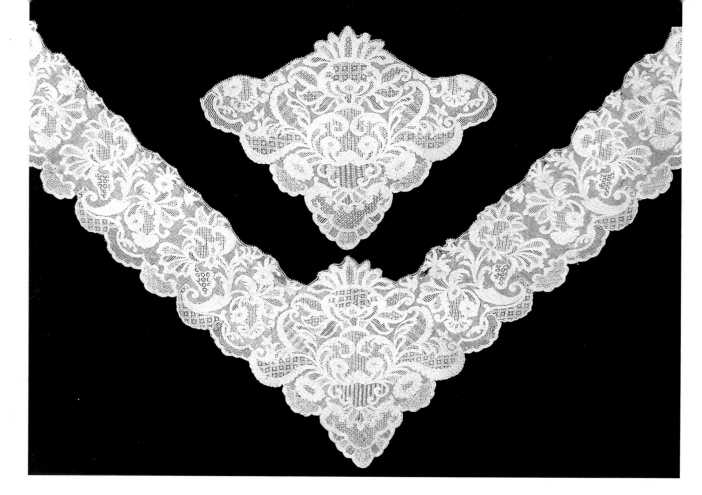

Dresden lace and the mid 18th century

What is immediately obvious about any Dresden lace, or embroidery as it should more properly be called, is the beauty and variety of its drawn-thread filling stitches. We have already seen that decorative fillings were becoming more prolific in various media in the 1720s: the 'bizarre' silks, laces and related whiteworks all show examples, as does the Nottingham whiteworked apron with its fantastic birds (Plate II.30), but many of the earlier fillings differ from those in Dresden work. Some are arrays of florets or eyelets, others include drawn-work but were often worked in two stages: the muslin ground was first drawn to create a regular net and then this was patterned with needle-weaving or other

Plate II.41 Detail of two corners from a Dresden-worked handkerchief (the muslin centre has been cut away and a picot edging added at a later date)

This, like several of the lappets seen previously, is an appliqué work, the dense parts of the design being created by two layers of fabric outlined with couched threads. The astonishing difference is that all the spaces around and between the dense areas are filled with drawn-thread work and even some of the dense areas themselves are embellished. The central design comprises a 'palmette', a composition of stylised flowers, leaves and scrolls about a vertical axis of symmetry, similar in character to the palmette in the lace-patterned silk in Plate II.34.

stitching. Dresden fillings, on the contrary, are normally worked in a single process: the embroidery thread is worked systematically across the surface of the fabric to create both openings and surface work simultaneously in geometric patterns that vary from one area to the next. The whole task requires meticulous counting of threads to maintain the regularity of patterning, a task difficult enough on modern fabrics, one would think impossible on the ultra-fine muslins used during the 18th century.

Although some earlier fillings were worked differently, the Dresden technique was already known by the early 18th Century. It may even have originated in Germany as early as the Middle Ages as embroideries known as 'opus Teutonicum' use counted-thread techniques but, not having studied these, the first positive example I can cite is in a Swedish sampler, initialled and dated CMS 1678, in the Nordiska Museum, Stockholm: an illustration can be seen in Margaret Swain's book, 'Historical Needlework'.

The first dated example I can show is in an English sampler worked by Mary Harris and dated 1725 (Plates II. 42). This includes a number of areas worked solely with a square net of drawn-thread embroidery together with areas of net overworked in a subsequent process such as we have seen on several 'tree-of-life' designs but it also includes more complex stitches worked in a single process. It is impossible to say whether the techniques used in this sampler were developed independently here, in England, or imported from the Continent. Bearing in mind the widespread nature of embroidery in the period and the various ways in which it was used to copy lace, as demonstrated by the lappets and cap crowns already discussed, it is more than likely that the new development arose in a number of different places simultaneously but that Saxony offered the right conditions for it to flower in the early 18th century. At that time Germany was divided into a number of wealthy principalities with a cultured aristocracy linked to the major Royal families of Europe but it also had a flourishing merchant class. The former was able to buy the finest laces while the latter had their example before their eyes and, no doubt, a desire to emulate them.

Plate II.41a *Detail of the kerchief in Plate II.41 showing some of the variety of drawn-thread filling stitches used.*

Plate II.42 *Major part of an English sampler worked by Mary Harris in 1725: sadly, the edges are very degraded and discoloured.*

Mary Harris's sampler is a true sampler, a record of stitches for use in later works. Although the design of this sampler is of a vase of flowers rather than a tree, the treatment of the stems and placing of the vase on a mound recall the 'tree-of-life' designs. The petals are, however, much more rounded than in the designs in Plates II.26-II.30 and even the pointed leaves have wide bases, all providing spaces for the lace-like fillings. Although many fillings are worked in the 'Dresden' manner, they are not as fine as in true Dresden laces. The stems and other solid parts of the design are filled in with darning stitches just like those in the tree-of-life designs but not common in true Dresden work. The outlines are worked in blanket stitch in a manner rarely seen elsewhere, with some lines in chain stitch.

The V&A holds an English sampler signed and dated 'Elizabeth Morley 1712' with a similar vase–of-flowers design but worked entirely in needlepoint lace stitches: the flowers are less well drawn than here but the design includes various filling stitches and three exotic birds.

Plate II.42a (right top)
Detail of the sampler in Plate II.42 showing the date, 1725, and name, HARRIS, embroidered over a pre-worked drawn-thread net.

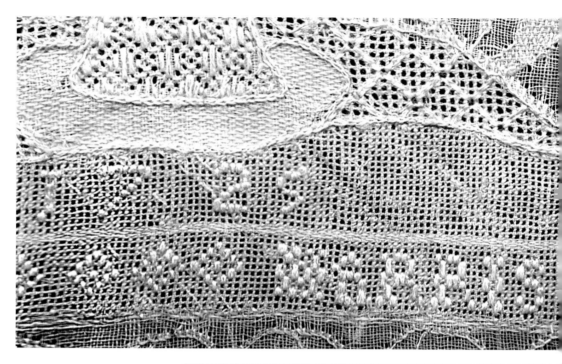

Plate II.42b (right bottom)
Detail of the sampler in Plate II.42 showing stems and some petals in darning stitch, outlines in chain stitch and blanket stitch and drawn-thread fillings including a simple drawn-thread net. Two embroidery threads are used, one being a shiny, untwisted linen.

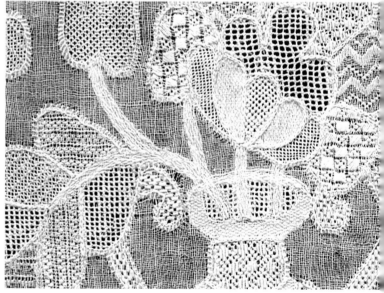

Although the beginnings of the Dresden industry are unclear, records indicate that whitework embroidery was being worked professionally in Saxony by the 1710s and, by the 1720s, the embroideresses were developing a proficiency in whitework to be unmatched in any other part of Europe. They applied their skills not just to caps and lappets but to handkerchiefs, aprons, sleeve ruffles, men's shirt frills and any other trimming where lace might alternatively be used. Although no doubt initially developed for the home market, Dresden work soon gained such renown that it was exported throughout Europe and bought by the most wealthy and aristocratic, being acceptable wear as a substitute for lace even for some formal occasions.

The incredible quantity of openwork fillings used in Dresden work certainly give it the appearance of lace but what is perhaps surprising is that, unlike the designs of the caps and lappets seen in Plates II.36–II.40, its designs were not close copies of lace or other fabric designs of the period.

During her work in setting up a major exhibition of Dresden work a few years ago, Dr. Ruth Bleckwenn investigated this question in depth and found a number of discrepancies between the motifs used in the two techniques and also in the way they were linked. In her catalogue of the exhibition★, Dr. Bleckwenn posits that this is because the embroidery, as indicated above, was developed to satisfy the wants of the German bourgeois classes, a group with sufficient culture to want luxury products but rather conservative tastes. The result is a textile which follows the general design trends of the 18th century but perhaps with a slight time-lag compared with the high-fashion scene and which has a distinctive character of its own. As we have seen, one style in vogue in woven fabrics in the 1720s was the so-called 'lace-pattern' (Plate II.34) which included complex arrangements of flowers and foliage surrounding symmetrical palmette designs. Although lace-makers, usually working in narrow bands, rarely imitated this style completely, embroideresses did not face the same restrictions. Like lace, Dresden work was extremely time-consuming to make and is found almost exclusively as borders on costume accessories but it had one major advantage over lace: it was worked on the article being made, not as a separate edging. It was therefore very much easier to vary both the width of a border and its pattern. The result was that palmette designs, rare in lace, could spread from the corners of aprons and handkerchiefs towards their centres. There they were not surrounded by foliage as in woven silks; instead the foliage patterns spread away symmetrically on either side of the palmettes to form borders along the edges of the article (see Plate II. 43). This design arrangement, once established, was so successful that it continued in use for the rest of the 18th century even though the palmette motifs eventually degenerated into simple floral sprays and, except in furnishing fabrics, its progenitor in woven textiles was wholly superseded by other designs.

The 1730s-40s brought further developments in the woven silk industries. The ribbons linking the foliage and floral motifs disappeared from many woven silks only to reappear again in the later 1750s. Motifs initially grew larger and were set against clearer grounds, and more naturalistic European flowers and foliage were introduced, particularly into English fabrics. The French silk weavers also developed a method of intermixing and shading colours that made their designs appear much more three-dimensional than previously. This effect could not be copied in either lace or whitework and, whereas complex geometric patterning became less important in woven fabrics, embroideresses and lacemakers continued to enliven their works with fancy fillings.

The designs of Dresden work and woven fabrics therefore diverged but, as Dr. Bleckwenn points out, it was not just the arrangement of motifs within Dresden designs that differed from other textiles but the motifs themselves. In particular she picks out a few shapes as being especially common in Dresden work. One is a large composite flower with a roughly oval centre surrounded by sepals and petals, some worked in dense stitching, others filled with decoration (see Plate II.46a); these are not often seen in silks and laces, or at least not as main motifs, but are occasionally found in printed fabrics of the period. These shapes are undoubtedly seen in many of the examples illustrated in the Dresden catalogue which was drawn from major collections in Dresden, Hamburg and St. Gallen, Switzerland, among others, but are by no means so common in British collections. Another flower with an oriental lily-like shape (Plate II.45a), perhaps related to

---

★*'Dresdner Spitzen – Point de Saxe: Virtuose Weißstickerein des 18. Jahrhunderts' by Professor Ruth Bleckwenn, published by the Staatliche Kunstsammlungen Dresden, Kunstgewerbemuseum, Dresden, in 2000, referred to below as the 'Dresden Catalogue'.*

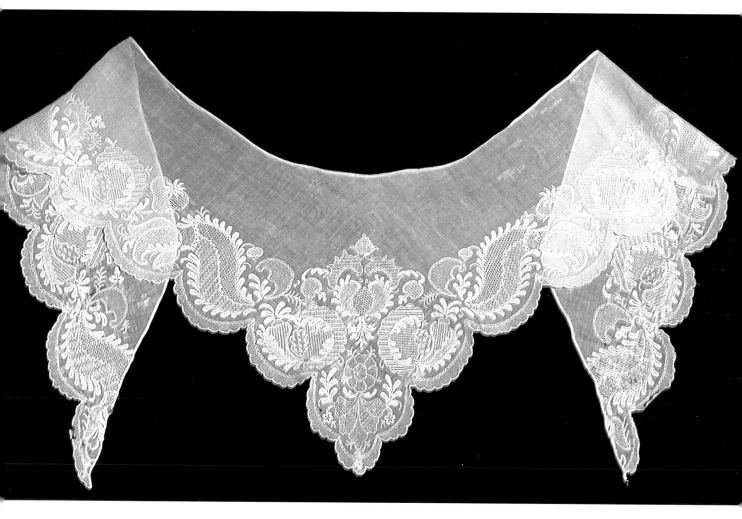

Persian designs but again differing from those in silks and laces, is more common in British collections while leaves with strong C- or S-shaped curvature, often with indented outlines (Plate II.43), and fruits, particularly stylised pomegranates and pears or strawberries (Plate II.43a), are common in all collections and have their counterparts in woven silks and laces of the first half of the 18th century.

Plate II.43 Mid-18th century Dresden-work kerchief with a palmette design in the corner and a design of large, stylised leaves, flowers and fruits spreading away symmetrically from it towards the corners, all within an outer, narrow border of drawn-thread work.
The design is similar in style and scale to that of Mary Strickland's kerchief (Plate II.44).
This kerchief may have been altered as the pattern continues into the rolled edges. (See p65 for a detail).

Plate II.44 *Portrait of Mary Strickland (1723-1765) who married Michael Blount in 1740; portrait c1740, artist unknown. Photograph reproduced courtesy of J.J. Eyston, The Mapledurham Trust. © The Mapledurham Trust, 2008.*

This is one of very few portraits that show the use of whiteworked accessories unambiguously and in sufficient detail for the pattern to be discerned. Mary is wearing a superb muslin kerchief and matching double sleeve ruffles decorated with Dresden work. Both accessories have scalloped edges with a narrow, continuous band of decoration immediately inside the edge and a broader band of flowing, floral decoration with large-scale motifs within that. Mary's cap may also be trimmed with Dresden work.

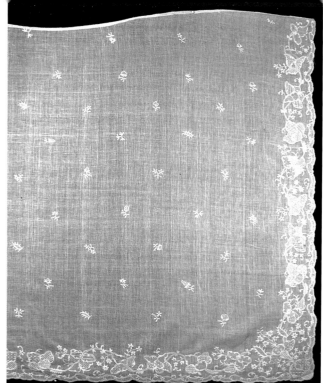

Plate II.45 (above) *Detail showing just over half a mid-18th century apron with a Dresden work border: the design of the other half of the apron is a mirror-image of that shown, including the fillings. The border again bears similarities to those on Mary Strickland's accessories: it has a 1/2in deep outer drawn border and an inner flowing design of large stylised flowers but this is quite open and delicate flower sprays spring from the larger flowers. The ground has diagonal rows of tiny sprigs (3/4in max.) but even some of these have drawn-thread fillings. It probably dates from the third quarter of the 18th century. W - 50.5in (128cm): Ls - 36in (91.5cm); Lc - 33in (84cm) (See p66 for a detail and p136 for pattern).*

Plate II.43a (left) *Detail of the kerchief in Plate II.43 showing typical stylised flowers, an S-shaped leaf and a strawberry-like fruit. The dense work is in buttonholed satin stitch, the outlines in chain stitch, and the outer edge is worked with inverted blanket stitch, leaving tufts of fabric projecting like picots. The large spaces within the design are filled with a wealth of drawn-thread fillings but the ground is plain except in the outer border.*

We see that true Dresden work is distinguished from other textiles of its period by its designs but it is also differentiated to a limited extent by its stitches. As we saw earlier, stitches can be separated into those used to form dense parts of a design and those used for outlining and edging. In Dresden work, the dense work is usually created by the application of a second layer of muslin, by shadow work or by buttonholed satin stitch, with application work being less common in later works. Darning stitch is hardly ever used. Lines and outlines are often in chain stitch, sometimes in stem stitch or couched threads, but the beauty of the work lies in the contrasts between the denser areas and the multitude of airy fillings. Occasionally these even cover the entire background to the pattern.

Having seen the beginnings of the Dresden style in the 1720s-30s, one would like to follow its development through into the later part of the century but this is very difficult to do. In the introduction to the Dresden catalogue, Dr. Bleckwenn compares various aspects of Dresden work designs, such as the use of meandering stems, scrolling tendrils, ribbons, cartouches and rosette flowers, with their use in other textiles but shows that many variations of the designs developed in parallel over the fifty years in which production was at its height and change was slow. It is therefore difficult to separate the various strands and devise rules for a chronology.

Plate II.45a *Detail from the corner of the apron in Plate II.45. The four (three shown) slightly different large flowers in the scrolling main border are typical of the stylised, oriental, lily-like flowers found in Dresden designs. There are two complete pattern repeats along the sides and one and a half repeats mirror-imaged along the bottom. Dense work is in shadow stitch; stems are in chain stitch and a form of ladder stitch; the edge also has a row of holes with chain stitch along the inside and blanket stitch along the outside. The fillings are non-repetitive but used symmetrically.*

Plate II.46 (below) *Dresden-work sleeve ruffle (the upper, straight edge is missing). This shows another common form of Dresden design: it has no narrow outer border of openwork; instead the edge is filled with a series of large flower and cartouche or cloud formations from which stems carrying large flower heads, leaves and buds spring into the main body of the ruffle. The design flows continuously from one end of the ruffle to the other, which is the most usual design form: less commonly, designs spread in opposite directions from a central, almost symmetrical pattern in the widest part of the ruffle.*
D - 5.4in (13.8cm); min.
D - 2.5in (6.4cm);
L - 34.5in (87.6cm).

Plate II.46a (above) *Detail of the ruffle in Plate II.46. Dense areas, including lines, are in shadow work, some outlines in chain stitch; the edge is rolled and held by blanket stitch. Notably, the entire ground is drawn: the same stitch is used throughout. The main flower shown, with its shaped centre surrounded by petals and sepals, is one of the flower forms picked out by Ruth Bleckwenn as common in Dresden laces.*

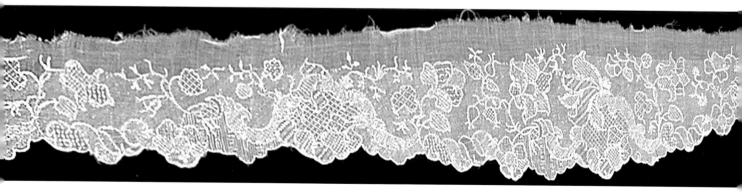

One reason for the slowness in change in the Dresden industry is that it was the beauty, variety and intricacy of its fillings that made it so desirable. To display the virtuosity of their stitching the embroideresses needed large spaces in the designs and these were provided by the large motifs of the 1720s-30s. These therefore continued in use well into the second half of the century whereas, in other textile fields, there was a much quicker progression towards sparser designs, with smaller, more tenuous and discrete motifs which provided much less room for fillings.

Another reason for the slow change is apparent from a study of a wide range of examples and is also commented upon by Dr. Bleckwenn: this was the manner in which many embroideries were designed. Time and again, similar motifs recur in slightly varying combinations and arrangements from one

Plate II.47 *Portrait of Mary Newman by Thomas Beach (© Witt Library, The Courtauld Institute of Art, London). This portrait is reputed to have been painted in 1768 but shows Mary Newman wearing costume including a Dresden-worked kerchief and sleeve ruffles very similar to those of Mary Strickland in Plate II.44. Mary Newman is depicted as an elderly lady so it is not surprising to see her wearing dress of an earlier period. Dresden work of this quality, though cheaper than lace, was an expensive luxury and would have been preserved carefully, perhaps worn only on special occasions.*

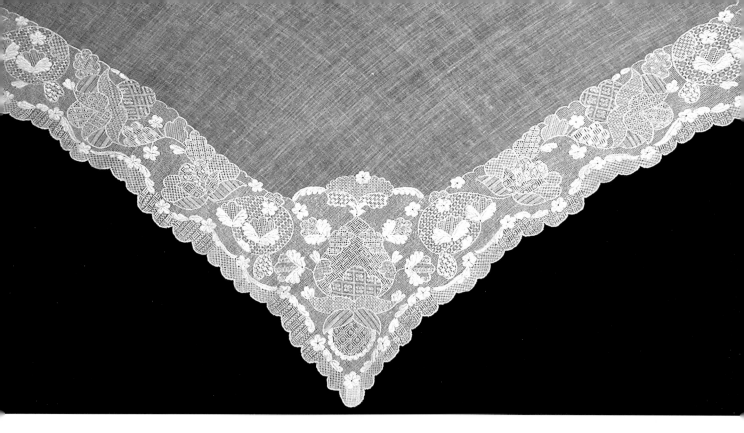

article to another, some results being more successful than others. Although the Dresden industry employed some skilled designers, untrained personnel could achieve acceptable results by drawing on earlier patterns, taking one motif from here, another from there and combining them on a 'mix-and-match' basis, this process possibly continuing over decades★. The three 'water lily' designs in Plates II.48 – II.50 illustrate this point: a sleeve ruffle with a fairly similar design may be seen in the Temple Newsam collection, Leeds.

A further complicating factor is that copies were made in many other countries, which may be the case in one or more of the examples in Plates II.48 – II.50. Dresden work is therefore difficult to date precisely. The best one can say is that, if one sees a design feature in a Dresden lace which is distinctly similar to that of a lace or other textile of known date, then the Dresden work is likely to be of the same date or slightly later.

Plate II.48 Detail of the corner of a kerchief with a 'water lily' design. The main flower, which is perhaps a stylised water lily, is best seen in the border where it is inclined at about 45° to the edge but the extreme delicacy of the work, particularly the very fine outlining in chain stitch, make it difficult to differentiate the water lilies from the adjacent cloud-like motifs.

The pattern does not repeat exactly along the edges and the fillings are not used symmetrically as in the best Dresden work. Dense pattern - buttonholed satin stitch; edge - inverted blanket stitch with picot-like tufts.

Ls – 31in, 31.5in (79cm, 80cm); D (corner pattern) – 8.5in (21.5cm). (See p71 for detail).

★We know few names in this field but, in the Dresden Catalogue, Ruth Bleckwenn records one designer, Friedrich Siegmund Petterlins, who was originally employed by the Meissen porcelain factory but subsequently provided designs for Dresden whitework.

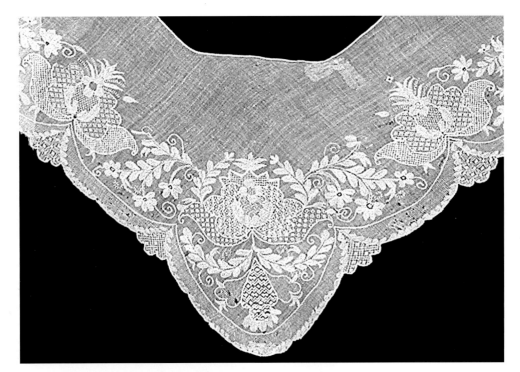

Plate II.49 (left) *Detail of the corner of a second kerchief with a 'water lily' design. Here a slightly different version of the 'water lily' is used in the corner with a variant repeated in the border: its upright orientation gives a very different feel to the design from that in Plate II.48. The design is unusual in having an upright, symmetrical motif in the border although this does alternate with a flowing, asymmetric design. Dense pattern - darned; lines - chain and blanket stitches; edge - buttonholed. The border scallops are filled with drawn-thread work except at the ends. Ls − 34in, 35in (86.5cm, 89cm); D(corner pattern) − 8.5in (21.5cm).*

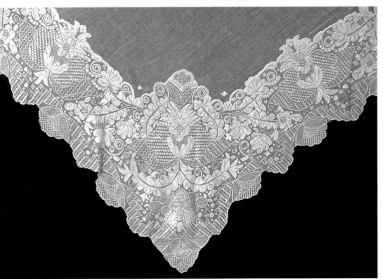

Plate II.50 (left) *Detail of the corner of a third kerchief with a 'water lily' design.: Accession No. T9834, Blaise Castle House Museum, Bristol. The 'water lily' in this kerchief is very similar to that in Plate II.49 as, indeed, is the rest of the main border design, but the use of different stitches and inclusion of additional motifs to fill spaces in the design makes this difficult to discern. The design is further confused by the elaborate outer border which contains an inverted miniature version of the water lily. In Plate II.49 the design is seen much more clearly against the plain ground and with the neat outer border. Dense pattern - buttonholed satin stitch; lines - chain stitch and couched threads; edge - inverted blanket stitch with picot-like tufts. The embroidery has been cut from its original fabric and remounted on a larger triangular panel of muslin. Ls − 33.5in, 34.5in (85cm, 87.5cm), probably 3in (7.5cm) shorter originally.*

Despite the underlying conservatism of the Dresden industry, designs did change in tune with the fashions of the day and, in 1770, the French designer Saint-Aubin was still able to say, in his work 'L'Art du Brodeur', that 'Les Saxonnes imitent assez bien les dessins des plus belles dentelles; leur Broderie en fil plat sur mousseline, est la plus délicate & la plus correcte que nous connoissions dans ce genre.'★ By the 1780s, however, fashion was content with much simpler embroideries. The market for Dresden work had already been reduced by competition from imitative industries, particularly those of Denmark and Dinant, in modern Belgium, but also by copies made by amateurs and professionals throughout Europe. The new fashions could be supplied more easily by home industries and the Dresden market dwindled rapidly. Some Saxon embroideresses turned their hands to tambouring or other lighter forms of embroidery but, by 1800, the industry, which had employed thousands of workers, was effectively dead.

It is sad to think of the death of an industry but, when Dresden work was at its peak, it was copied not only throughout Europe but also in her colonies. Many of the imitations were for home consumption but there were also notable export industries This makes it extremely difficult to distinguish true Dresden work from embroideries from other sources: only occasionally do signed and dated examples or embroideries with a specific regional character enable us to differentiate between them. We shall therefore return to the mid century to see some examples of the competing products but, before doing so, another beautiful Dresden worked kerchief displayed on a costume from the Devonshire Collection of Period Costume, Totnes follows.

★ (The embroideresses of Saxony imitate the designs of the most beautiful laces quite well: their embroidery in flat thread on muslin is the most delicate and perfect of this type that we know).

Plate II.48a Further detail of the kerchief in Plate II.48.

Plate II.50a Further detail of the kerchief in Plate II.50.

Plate II.51 *Dresden-worked handkerchief displayed on a costume from the Devonshire Collection of Period Costume, Totnes.*

This example shows a different style of Dresden design in which a decorated ribbon runs through the border: it probably dates from about 1750-70.

The stylised flowers and formal design of the kerchief are contrasted with the much more naturalistic, playful rendering of flowers and bows on the brocaded silk, the former being typical of Dresden-work designs, the latter of English ones.

The silk dates from about the late 1740s-50s (see Plate II.56c for a detail): the robe style is slightly later, probably altered from its original form.

1753-89 REYNOLDS AT HEIGHT OF CAREER
1754 THOMAS CHIPPENDALE'S 'THE GENTLEMAN & CABINET MAKER'S DIRECTOR'
1755 JOHNSON'S 'DICTIONARY OF THE ENGLISH LANGUAGE'
1756-63 SEVEN YEARS WAR GIVES ENGLAND NAVAL SUPREMACY
1757 BATTLE OF PLESSEY, INDIA
1758 ROBERT ADAM SETS UP FAMILY FIRM IN LONDON
1759 QUEBEC CAPTURED BY GEN. JAMES WOLFE

The mid-late 18th century

By the 1740s Britain was importing so much whitework from Germany that, in the early 1750s, various English, Irish and Scottish Societies offered prizes to those producing the finest imitations of Dresden work: in 1753, for example, a Mrs. Maria Maule received a prize of five guineas for the best pair of men's ruffles, one of fourteen pairs of 'very curious men's needlework ruffles' submitted to the Anti-Gallican Society of Scotland.

Attempts were also made to mechanise the embroidery process and, in 1755, K.F. Weisenthal was granted a patent for a double-pointed needle that created stitches almost identical to hand-made ones. Unfortunately this was ahead of its time: it was not until the 19th century that a machine utilising the same principle was commercially successful.

In Britain, naturally, we can expect to find many examples of

Plate II.52 Half handkerchief worked by Rachel Leonard of Norton, Massachusetts and including the date 1752 and her initials worked in eyelet holes in the centre of a flower near one corner. The dense areas are worked in shadow stitch and buttonholed satin stitch while outlines are in chain stitch.
CB – 31 11/16in (80.5cm); Ls – 52 3/8in (133cm). (Plain weave cotton embroidered with cotton; Museum of Fine Arts, Boston, USA; American, Colonial, 1752; gift of Mrs. Susan Hedge Davis of Plymouth, Mass., 12.193).
Photograph © 2008 Museum of Fine Arts, Boston, USA.

locally-produced whitework but the next dated example (Plate II.52) comes from America: it is a kerchief intitialed and dated RL 1752 and is housed in the Museum of Fine Arts, Boston, Massachusetts.

Fortunately the museum also has an embroidered coat of arms from the same source worked with 'Rachel Leonard aged 13 1740' so that we know that Rachel was about 25 when she worked the kerchief. The work includes the usual palmette design in the corner, an inner border of large flowers carried on flowing stems interspersed with small leaves, and an outer border of cloud-like shapes. All are worked in the customary Dresden manner with buttonholed satin stitch, shadow work, chain stitch and a variety of drawn fillings: there is little to distinguish this from the Dresden original.

Although few other dated accessories have come to light from the late 18th century, there are rather more dated patterns and illustrations. For example, pen-and-ink sketches survive showing designs for a cap and lappet drawn in about 1761 by Henrietta Cumming, governess to the children of the Scottish Lord Balcarres★. The lappet includes large S-shaped leaves which occupy its full width, together with a large cartouche at the lower end and various florets and fanciful shapes arranged around them. The whole is more reminiscent of lace designs of the 1730s than of 1760 whereas a roughly contemporary corner design by one of her pupils, Lady Margaret Lindsay, is very much lighter in character, including finely-drawn curving swags which even scroll round the corner, leaving no room for the usual symmetrical palmette.

A design held in the prints and drawings collection of the V&A has, on the reverse, the inscriptions 'a border for ruffles 1764' and 'Miss Saymors pattern Somersetshire' (Plate II.53). The design is fairly clumsily drawn but includes asymmetric floral sprays rising from a border of tiny cartouches and leaf shapes that provide spaces for fancy fillings. This is reminiscent of French needlepoint designs of the 1760s-70s (see Plate II.54) but the more sophisticated whiteworked fragment shown in Plate II.55 is much more clearly modelled on such laces: the expanse of drawn-work, creating a clear net ground, adds to its lace-like quality. When we look at items, such as the ruffle in Plate II.55, that do not have a specifically German character, we find vast differences in the quality of workmanship. Plate II.56, for

Plate II.53 (opposite top) Drawing of a pattern held in the prints and drawings collection of the V&A, Box T10A, No.E 344/5, inscribed on the reverse 'a border for ruffles 1764' and, beneath that, 'Miss Saymors pattern Somersetshire'.

Plate II.54 (opposite centre) French needlepoint border with the Alençon net ground. The chronology of fashion changes in high-class laces through the 18th century is clearly established so that this border can be dated with reasonable accuracy to about the 1760s. French needlepoints, like Dresden work, relied to some extent on a variety of fillings for their beauty and so also retained cartouches and other shapes that could accommodate them in their designs. The late 1750s-70s saw a vogue for border patterns including cartouches from which floral sprays spring towards the opposite edge and spread asymmetrically in opposite directions, the motifs gradually becoming lighter with less use of fillings through the period.

example, shows a very different but superb apron patterned with an array of delightful floral arrangements of recognisable flowers: this is displayed on a costume from the Devonshire Collection of Period Costume, Totnes. Although undated, the apron is so similar to that worn by Lady Howe in her portrait by Gainsborough in about 1760 (Plate II.57) that it is surely of the same vintage. The realism of the flower forms is, however, the only hint of naturalism: flowers and leaves that are totally unrelated to each other in real life are carried on the same stalks and, as in Dresden work, the spaces formed by the outlines are used simply to accommodate a variety of filling stitches. The quality of this apron might suggest a German origin but the flowers are not part of the usual Dresden repertoire: it is most probably of English professional manufacture.

★ *see 'Scottish Embroidery: Medieval to Modern' by M. Swain for illustrations.*

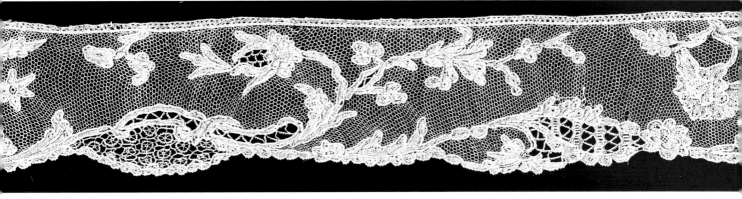

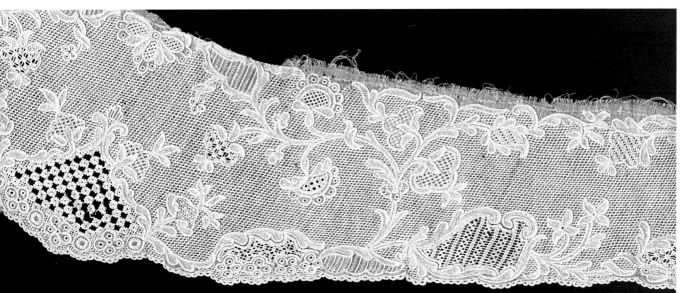

Plate II.55 *Fragment of a sleeve ruffle in whitework imitating a French needlepoint of about the 1760s. Here it is not just the design that is imitated: the ground is also completely embroidered in drawn-thread work and the outlines of the design are strongly emphasised, copying the heavy, raised outlines of French needlepoints. The fillings, particularly the very open one on the left, are also similar to needlepoint fillings: the close simulation achieved suggests that this may itself be a French product.*

75

Plate II.56 *Apron and kerchief shown on a robe from the Devonshire Collection of Period Costume, Totnes: the back of the same robe is shown in Plate II.51.*

The apron is patterned with three different floral sprays arranged in a regular array across the plain ground of diaphanous muslin; there is a very simple, narrow border pattern. The sprays are in a distinctly rococo style, similar to that of the fabric on which it is shown, but the woven flowers are treated very naturalistically (see Plate II.56c) whereas the shapes of the whiteworked flowers are used primarily as vehicles for the filling stitches.

The silk is probably of earlier date than the apron: the gown has been remodelled in the 1760s, the sleeves in particular being restyled with falling cuffs. The kerchief has a woven design and lace edging: it is shown in greater detail in Plate II.60. It is sufficiently large for the corners to be passed round the waist and tied at the back, a style of wear that was to become more common later in the century.

Apron: W - 36in (91.5cm) (1 fabric width – other half missing); Ls - 40 in (101.5cm); Lc −34.25 in (87cm) (possibly shortened): worked mainly in chain stitch and drawn-thread work.

1760 George III succeeds

1760-84 Gainsborough at height of career

1761 Clive made Governor of Bengal

1762 Rousseau's 'Contrat Social' and 'Emile'

1764 James Hargreaves' 'spinning jenny' mechanises spinning of cotton weft

1765-85 Watt improved steam engines

1768-71 Cook's first journey to Tahiti and Australia

1769 Wedgewood's new works 'Etruria'

Plate II.56a (right top) Detail of one of the floral sprays from the apron in Plate II.56 together with part of the border. In these floral sprays the stems have been reduced to narrow lines worked in double rows of chain stitch. The denser parts of the designs are also filled in with chain stitch while the outlines are in single lines of chain stitch.

Plate II.56b (below) Detail of another of the floral sprays from the apron in Plate II.56.

Plate II.56c (right bottom) Detail of the silk fabric of the robe in Plates II.51 and II.56. The trailing cords tied into bows and asymmetric flower sprays are typically rococo in character.

Plate II.57 Mary Countess Howe by Thomas Gainsborough, *c1760 from the Iveagh Bequest, Kenwood (© English Heritage Photo Library).*

Over her pink silk open robe with matching petticoat, Lady Howe wears a diaphanous white muslin apron decorated with floral sprays which appear to be similar in character to those in Plates II.56-56b. The details of the floral border pattern are unclear.

A muslin handkerchief is also worn round the neck; the ends are brought down the front of the bodice and crossed, possibly being caught under the waistband of the apron to keep them in place. The wide, flowing, triple sleeve ruffles appear to be of lace or, at least, are trimmed with lace rather than whitework.

Although this book is dedicated primarily to whitework embroideries, I cannot resist including one apron with a mixture of whitework and coloured embroidery (Plate II.58). This is clearly amateur work: the drawing of the flower sprays is not very elegant and the embroidery is not well executed but the overall effect is charming. What is also interesting is the placing of the flower sprays in plain lozenges defined by lozenges filled with a vermicular pattern: vermicular designs had been very popular in the first half of the 18th century when they were used particularly as backgrounds to floral designs (see Plate III.16). Diaper and similar geometric designs, on the other hand, became popular in the 1750s –1760s and are seen particularly in the coarser, poorer-quality laces used for large costume accessories such as the capes that were fashionable then. One example can be seen in Plate IV.45, p166, whereas another white apron with a lozenge, or diaper, design can be seen in the portrait of the Bateson family in Plate II.59.

Plate II.58 (above) *Apron gathered and bound into a linen tape at the top.*
The vermicular patterns in alternate lozenges are worked in backstitch while the floral patterns are created by appliqué work sewn with a
bright pink thread. The stitching is irregular and confused but lines appear to be mainly in stem stitch with extra stitches worked over some
lines and looking rather like thorns; some of these hold the cut edges of the fabric while others form fancy fillings in the flower centres. The
scale of the design is very similar to that of Lady Howe's apron, suggesting a date for this article of about the 1760s, although the Bateson
girls, at about the same date, had designs on a smaller scale.
W – 55in (147cm) (1.5 fabric widths) bound into 16.5in (42cm) at the top: Ls – 40.5in (103cm); Lc - 35.75in (91cm). The edges are rolled.
(See p136 for pattern).

Plate II.58a (top right) *Detail of the apron in Plate II.58 showing the simple stitching in pink thread.*

While considering geometric designs, we can return to the kerchief shown on the robe in Plate II.56 and also in Plate II.60. This combines a diaper-patterned centre with a floral border and has an added bobbin lace edging. At first sight the main panel appears to be embroidered but closer inspection shows it to be woven in imitation of whitework. The dense design is created by supplementary weft threads of thicker, looser yarn than the fine ground yarn; they are inserted solely where needed to create the pattern and are cut off at the back. The openwork, on the other hand, is created by manipulation of the ground threads.

The floral design is just what one might expect of a Dresden-worked article; it includes corner designs that spread towards the centre and a narrower border pattern that is mirror imaged both about the corners and about the centres of each side. What it lacks is the complexity of early Dresden designs. The Temple Newsam collection, Leeds, also has a beautiful example of such work: this is an apron in natural blonde-coloured silk with a gauze ground (Catalogue No. 1949.008.093 – not illustrated). Its pattern includes a running border design and an array of two different sprigs oriented in opposite directions in alternate lines across the centre.

Plate II.58b *Detail of the apron in Plate II.58 showing one of the floral sprays and the vermicular patterning.*

Plate II.59 (opposite left) *Detail from a portrait, c1761, of the family of Thomas Bateson, Esq. 1705-91 attributed to Strickland Lowry, 1737- c85. (Ulster Museum, Belfast) Photograph reproduced courtesy the Trustees of National Museums Northern Ireland: © National Museums Northern Ireland 2008.*

The girl on the left is in a back-opening yellow robe, a common form of dress for children. Her diaphanous muslin accessories are trimmed with blue ribbons. The apron has a diaper design with a floret in each lozenge shape: it appears to have an added lace border. Her bodice front is also covered with a triangular layer of muslin with similar ribbon and lace trimming while her sleeve ruffles appear to be of plain muslin with lace edgings. Her younger sister is similarly attired but in a blue dress, her apron being decorated with floral sprigs arranged in rows and columns but without the diaper setting of the older girl's. The floral sprays on both aprons are much smaller and less elaborate than Lady Howe's but almost contemporary. It is impossible to be certain what technique was used to create the apron designs: woven muslins imitating whitework embroidery were being made by this date as seen in Plate II.60.

The floral sprigs are painted so variably that they were most likely embroidered but the diaper ground might have been woven.

Plate II.60 (above) *Handkerchief with a woven pattern imitating Dresden work, c1750-70: this is also seen on the robe in Plate II.56. This handkerchief is slightly unusual in having a central design: the majority of 18th-century kerchiefs have only border patterns, all-over patterns being reserved for aprons, but there was a fashion in the third quarter of the 18th century for capes and similar accessories in lace with diaper or similar geometric patterns. The lace trimming of the handkerchief is of Valenciennes bobbin lace dating from about the 1750s: the handkerchief as a whole is probably contemporary. (See over for details).*

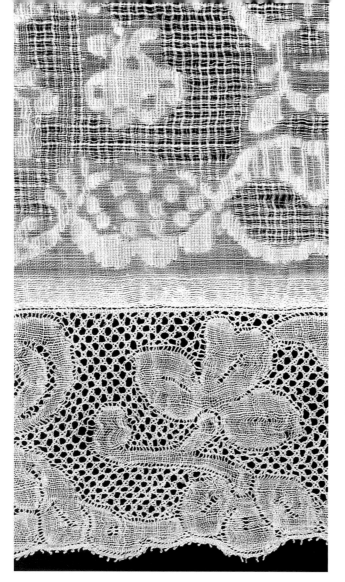

Plate II.60b Detail of the reverse of the handkerchief in Plate II.60. In this portion of the kerchief, the thicker supplementary weft threads run parallel to the direction of the design on the border. They are introduced solely where needed for the pattern and are cut off at the back of the work.

Plate II.60a Detail of the right side of the handkerchief in Plate II.60. The thicker threads that create the denser parts of the design are supplementary wefts and run in parallel throughout the kerchief: in this part of the border, the weft threads are perpendicular to the border. The direction of needle-run embroidery threads varies from area to area. The more open areas which look like drawn-thread work are created by the weave.

Still on the geometric theme, the design of the apron in Plate II.61 is based on a diaper pattern but worked in a very different technique from those discussed previously. This is tambour work, the chain stitch worked with a hooked needle introduced into Europe from the East in about the 1760s. Here the branching, leafy stems create rough lozenge shapes that accommodate florets and tulip heads in a design that is similar in scale to that of the older girl's apron in Plate II.59.

The tambour technique is ideally suited to creating linear designs but the love of filling stitches created by Dresden work did not die easily. The apron in Plate II.61 incorporates relatively few but that shown in Plate II.62, which is probably of about the same date or slightly later, still has a filled border pattern and larger corner motifs. It is unusually wide, being made from two widths of fabric, and displays a design of undulating stems extending vertically upwards and occasionally branching into leafy sprays. A page from 'The Lady's Magazine' for 1785 (Plate II.63) shows a pattern for a gown which includes a similar undulating, branching stem design combined with parallel bands of discrete flower heads and ladder-like designs. The patterning of the apron is a little more crowded than that of the magazine pattern, suggesting a slightly earlier date, but fabric designs incorporating alternating, vertical bands of different patterns were popular from the 1760s through into the 1790s.

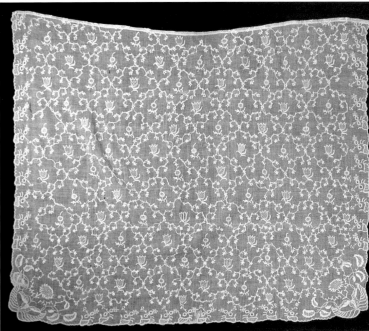

Plate II.61 (above) Apron with a tamboured design, c1760s-70s. This apron is worked largely in tamboured chain stitch in a very thick thread which gives a strong contrast with the fine muslin. Ls - 36in (89cm); Lc - 34in (86cm) (possibly shortened) W - 49in (125cm).

Plate II.61a (left) Detail of the apron in Plate II.61 showing tambour work creating both lines and denser areas of pattern. The work also includes overcast eyelets and drawn-thread fillings. The edge is finished with an added length of bobbin lace with picots.

Plate II.62 (below) *Apron with a tamboured design; c1760s-80s. The apron has a narrow border pattern, 3/8in — 3/4in deep, filled with a variety of drawn-thread fillings though their use is not as regular as in professional Dresden work: some differences in the tightness of working suggest more than one worker. The main ground is filled with nineteen sinuous, trailing stems extending from top to bottom; these include two alternating patterns which curve in opposite directions but are not carefully drawn. The stems adjacent the two side edges spring from motifs which replace the usual palmettes at the lower corners while flower sprigs occupy spaces between the trailing stems. W - 73in (188cm) (2 fabric widths): Ls − 43.5in (112cm); Lc - 39.25in (100cm) (See p137 for pattern).*

Plate II.62a (above) *A corner of the apron in Plate II.62.*

Plate II.63 (right) *Page from 'The Lady's Magazine' for 1785 showing 'A New Pattern for Working a Frock or Gown'. The pattern is arranged on the page with the bands of design extending horizontally but it would most likely have been worked with the bands extending vertically. The pattern is just as suitable for an apron as a gown.*

Plate II.62b (above) Further detail of the apron in Plate II.62.

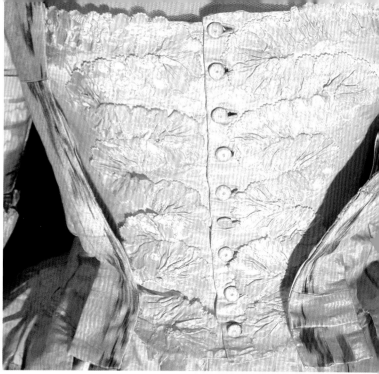

Plate II.64 Cream silk stomacher c late 1750s-60s displayed with an open robe from the Devonshire Collection of Period Costume, Totnes. The stomacher is made in two halves which button together for decorative effect. Each half is decorated with an applied sinuous trail of ruched silk ribbon of a colour matching that of the figured cream silk of the stomacher itself. The stomacher was probably made originally to match a robe as robes with matching stomachers were very popular in the third quarter of the 18th century: examples may be seen in Plates II.13 and II.65. The sinuous lines of decoration, like those of the embroidered apron in Plate II.62, are typical of the rococo period.

One subject of this work which has not yet been discussed in any detail is the woman's stomacher. Most true whitework stomachers appear to predate the 1760s and examples may be seen on pages 120-124 but, while we are considering accessories of about this period, I will include one stomacher that, although not embroidered in the sense we have been considering, relies on similar differences of light, shade and texture for its effect. This is an example from the Devonshire Collection of Period Costume and is shown in Plate II.64.

Returning to true whitework, Dresden work was still popular in the 1760s but, as we have seen, lighter designs and forms of embroidery were becoming fashionable. A further example is seen in a portrait of Lady Sarah March (Plate II.65) which can be dated by the dress and hairstyle to the late 1750s-60s. Lady Sarah's sleeve ruffles are decorated with a simple pattern of a sinuous leafy stem carrying tiny flower heads: a very similar ruffle is seen in Plate II.66.

*Plate **II.65** Portrait of Lady Sarah March, possibly by Cotes; late 1750s-60s. (© Witt Library, The Courtauld Institute of Art, London). Lady Sarah wears a silk robe with a stomacher dressed en échelle with graduated ribbon bows, with similar ribbons on her sleeves. Under the latter she wears very full, double muslin ruffles decorated with whitework embroidery and very narrow inner ruffles like those of Dorothy Quincy in her portrait in Plate II. 13. The character of the embroidery is extremely similar to that of the ruffle in Plate II.66. Lady Sarah's kerchief is of a very light black bobbin lace.*

The accessories shown in Plates II.52–II.66 demonstrate the wide variety of whitework designs current within the relatively short period of two decades but, together, indicate that design was becoming sparser than in the first half of the century. Whiteworks thus followed the general trend in fabric designs of the period, a trend which continued into the 1770s as designs broke up into isolated motifs. The V&A is fortunate in having another dated apron from this period (Plate II.67): it is worked with the initials 'S W' and the date 1774 in hair in minute stitches in the top left-hand corner. The initials stand for Sarah Walters who, sadly, died at the age of thirteen or fourteen.

Like earlier aprons, this apron has an arrangement of floral sprays across the centre but they are more delicately drawn and the border pattern, instead of being continuous, comprises a series of discrete sprigs similar to those scattered over the ground. The lightness of character is well suited to dress of the later 18th century.

Plate II.66 *Detail of one flounce of a double muslin sleeve ruffle with a design of a scrolling, branching stem carrying simple leaves and flower heads. The motifs are worked entirely in darning stitch with the lines in double running stitch. The flower centres are not drawn to form eyelets, a common embellishment in this type of work and seen in Lady March's ruffles in Plate II.65. The outer edge is rolled and neatened with buttonhole stitch. The inner edges of the two falls are rolled, gathered and overstitched to opposite edges of a linen band. No other stitches are used.*
Upper ruffle (not shown): D – 8.8in (22cm); D min. – 4in (10cm) Lower ruffle: D – 10in (25.5cm); D min. – 4.5in (11.5cm).

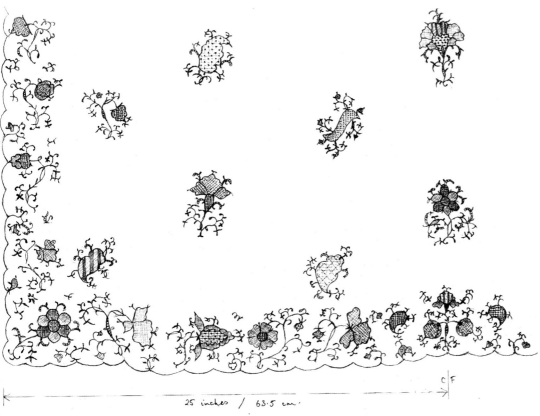

25 inches / 63·5 cm.

C|F

Plate II.67 Drawing of a
corner of an apron initialled
'SW' for Sarah Walters and
dated 1774; Catalogue
No. T105 – 1961, V&A.
The 27 sprays arranged in
staggered rows across the
ground include a mixture of
wild roses, stylised flowers and
fruits, and abstract shapes, thus
borrowing from the German
repertoire of Dresden work as
well as having English
features. The various shapes
house drawn-thread fillings.
The stems and outlines are
worked in chain stitch. The
scalloped edge is finished with
a form of ladder stitch with
blanket stitch on one side and
chain stitch on the other.
W – 49in (124.5cm);
Ls – 36.5in (92.7cm);
Lc – 38in(96.5cm).

As we move through the 1770s we see yet another design style
taking hold: this is the neo-classical style which, as already
noted, affected the shape and colour of everyday dress from the
1780s but was seen much earlier in architecture, portraiture and
the decorative arts. It is not, therefore, surprising that neo-
classical patterning should appear earlier in decorative fabrics
and my first roughly dated use in whitework is seen in a water-
colour illustration from Wimpole Hall, Cambridgeshire. The
complete picture, seen in Plate II.69, shows two ladies, in the
centre, attended by two women who, by their costumes, are of
lesser rank: the hats and hairstyles of the ladies date the images
to the late 1770s-early 1780s. It is interesting to note that the
difference in status is shown by the accessories and hair styles,
not by the women's robes: all wear robes in patterned fabrics,
three of striped material, with long full skirts uncluttered by
decoration: the only difference is that the backs of the skirts of
the central figures are slightly fuller and more raised at the waist.

1770 1st edition of 'The Lady's Magazine'
1771 Arkwright's water-powered mill in Derbyshire spins cotton warp
1773 Goldsmith's 'She Stoops to Conquer'
1774 Ban on wearing of printed cottons lifted
1774 Louis XVI succeeds in France
1775 Sheridan's 'The Rivals'
1775 - 1783 American war of independence
1776 Cavendish proves hydrogen is an element
1779 Cook killed in Hawaii on third journey
1779 Crompton's 'mule' spins a fine cotton warp: Britain's muslins now rival India's

Plate II.68 Detail of an
illustration from Wimpole Hall,
Cambridgeshire; reproduced
courtesy of The National Trust
for England and Wales;
©Georges Potirakis/NT.
The figures are painted in water
colours, cut out and pasted onto
a silk fabric. The woman on the
right wears an apron with a
diaper pattern but that of the
lady on the left includes a
scalloped border design and a
scattering of small floral sprigs
above an arrangement of
classical swags draped
symmetrically from ribbon bows
and extending in a deep band
across the bottom. Leaves and
sprigs are very tiny with little or
no room for filling stitches but
the playful nature of the rococo
has not been entirely lost. The
lady also has a handkerchief
decorated with coloured
embroidery draped over her arm.
(See p90 for full picture).

The two women on the right (Plate II.68) are most relevant
to our discussions so we shall look at these first. Both women
wear white aprons and kerchiefs but the lady on the left has
fuller sleeve ruffles, although these are narrow compared with
earlier ruffles: the woman on the right has slightly fuller robe
sleeves, probably with neat bands finishing her chemise sleeves
showing at the elbow. She also wears her white kerchief in a
neat, old-fashioned style, partly covered by a coloured
kerchief whereas the lady facing her has a much more
voluminous kerchief.

Most importantly as regards decoration, the lady's apron has a
fashionable design including neo-classical elements whereas the

subservient female wears an apron with a diaper pattern. As we
have seen, such geometric patterns were fashionable in the
1750s-60s but were somewhat outdated by the time of this
portrait. The apron could well have been passed on to her by
her mistress once it went out of fashion or she might have
worked it herself and worn it for many years.

Two examples of aprons with neo-classical features are shown
in Plates II.70 and II.71, the first having a simple linear design
with many similarities to that of the lady's apron but more
severely classical in style. The second retains the larger flowers
and complex filling stitches of the rococo period and probably
predates the portrait.

Plate II.69(above) *Two ladies (centre) and two women of lesser rank, painted in water colours, cut out and pasted onto a silk fabric.(Wimpole Hall, Cambridgeshire; reproduced courtesy of The National Trust for England and Wales; © Georges Potirakis/NT) The extremely full hairstyles and wide-brimmed hats of the central figures date this picture to the late 1770s-early 1780s. The more restrained hairstyles and caps of the other ladies are more suited to their obviously lower status. All four women wear white aprons and white kerchiefs, those of the two central ladies being much more voluminous than the others which are worn in a more severe, old-fashioned style. The woman on the right also wears a coloured kerchief. The simple striped decoration of the two aprons on the left contrasts with the more elaborate decoration of those on the right.*

Plate II.70 (opposite bottom) *Detail from an apron with a neo-classical design. The pattern includes 8 larger bows with dependent tassels supporting a laurel-leaf trail with smaller bows, tassels and dependent chains and swags of tiny leaves and florets. Around the edge is a typical classical border comprising a sinuous chain intertwined with a laurel-leaf trail. The edges themselves are all rolled. Although the neo-classical swag aspect of this design is similar to that of the lady's apron in Plates II.68 and II.69, its treatment is a little more severe. The straight edge, lack of flower sprigs dotted over the ground and simple border contribute to this severity, suggesting a later date for this apron, perhaps of the late 1780s or 1790s.*

The dense pattern and some lines are worked in whipped running stitches in thick, loosely twisted thread but the whipping often penetrates the fabric.

W - 51in (130cm): Ls – 40.5in (103cm); Lc – 35in (89); depth of bottom pattern – 8.25in (21cm) (See p137 for pattern).

Plate II.71 (above) *Detail of the lower part of an apron with a mixed rococo/neo-classical design.*
Although this apron has only a narrow border pattern and a plain field, its interest is created by two tiers of swags tied and supported at

three points by large ribbon bows with dependent tassels: the upper tier consists solely of filled leaf shapes and tiny sprigs but beneath them hang glorious trails of large flower heads with a multitude of fillings. The scale and intricacy of the flowers and foliage, which still have a certain rococo character, suggest that this apron may predate the portrait in Plate II.68.

The main stitch is chain stitch but some motifs are surrounded by an elaborate ladder stitch with blanket stitch along each side: the fillings are used indiscriminately in the pattern repeats. The top edge is turned to form a 3/8in (0.6cm) casing for a linen-tape draw-string - the edge pattern continues into the fold indicating possible shortening.

W - 53in (135cm): Ls and Lc – 30.25in (77cm).

91

Plate II.71a (left top) *Detail of Plate II.71 showing part of a floral swag.*

Plate II.72 (below) *Embroidery design from 'The Lady's Magazine' of 1785. The design is stated to be for an apron or handkerchief. It could easily have been worked by most amateurs either by needle-running or tambouring. Drawn-thread work could have been practised in the flower centres but would not have occupied much time compared with earlier designs.*

Classical swag designs, such as we have just seen, are suitable for wide expanses such as aprons but do not seem to have been used on smaller articles such as kerchiefs and ruffles: here the orientation of the swag design would not be appropriate. Instead, many ruffles continued to be worked with flowing border designs while, for kerchiefs, the earlier scheme of a larger corner motif and narrower borders was retained to the end of the century, with the differences that the design became ever more tenuous and the corner motifs became detached from the borders and lost their symmetry.

By the 1780s pocket books and fashion magazines showing not only the fashions of their time but also embroidery designs had become much more common and the next illustration is taken from such a source. It shows a pattern which includes an asymmetric spray of wheatears and flowers springing into the ground from the corner but totally separated from the flowering stem of the border design. The simple lines leave

little room for virtuosity of stitching: a similar design is seen on an apron worn in an allegory of Spring (Plate II.73).

Plate II.73 *Detail from an allegory of Spring from a series of engravings of the seasons by R. Dighton, c1785.*
A lady is shown seated in the countryside no doubt awaiting her beau in the carriage (not shown) in the background. Her stylish outfit, with its wide-brimmed hat over widely-dressed hair and buckled high-heeled shoes, includes a white kerchief under a black cloak. Single narrow ruffles trim her tight, elbow-length sleeves while a white muslin apron, with the embroidery design beautifully depicted, covers her skirt. The border design is similar to that in Plate II.72 but designs of this type were available in the new fashion magazines from the late 1770s through into the 1790s so that it is impossible to date surviving examples accurately. The apron includes our first example of a dotted ground, a very common feature of muslins from the 1780s into the early 19th century: an alternative to the dot was an extremely tiny flower head or sprig. (see Plates II.5 and II.22).

1780 GORDON RIOTS IN LONDON
1782 RUFFINI SET UP EDINBURGH EMBROIDERY WORKSHOP
1782–1812 MRS. SIDDONS AT HEIGHT OF ACTING CAREER
1784 WILLIAM PITT THE YOUNGER PRIME MINISTER
1786 MOZART'S 'MARRIAGE OF FIGARO'
1788 GEORGE HEPPLEWHITE'S 'CABINET-MAKER AND UPHOLSTERER'S GUIDE'
1789 FRENCH REVOLUTION

In the last quarter of the 18th century, another accessory that we have not so far seen became popular: this was the work bag, used for carrying not only equipment for sewing and other crafts but also pocket handkerchiefs, patch boxes, vinaigrettes or other such feminine necessities. These items might also be carried in pockets (see pages 124–126) under a lady's skirt until the slimmer line of the late 1790s made this inconvenient but patterns for work bags appeared in the magazines well before this as shown in Plates II.74 and II.75. These patterns may have been intended for coloured embroideries rather than whitework but the surviving whiteworked example shown in Plate II.76 demonstrates that white examples, even if lined in colour as in this case, were also used.

An Elegant Pattern for a Work Bag.

A New Pattern for a Work Bag.

Plate II.74 (above) Embroidery design from 'The Lady's Magazine' of 1778 described as 'An Elegant Pattern for a Work Bag'. (from a bound 1778 volume of the magazine in Exeter University Library).

Plate II.75 (left) Embroidery design from 'The Lady's Magazine' of 1785 described as 'A New Pattern for a Work Bag'. It is interesting that this pattern has a large, rococo-style central motif and an unrepetitive, flowing border design whereas the earlier pattern in Plate II.74 has a smaller, simpler motif and repetitive, if rather crowded border: one might expect the opposite from their dates.

Plate II.76 (above left) Whiteworked muslin work bag with a pink silk lining and pink silk ribbon draw string. The large floral design is in the rococo manner but is not very elegant and is worked in simple stitching in coarse thread. A band of bobbin-made net, of drochel type, is caught to the edge at intervals so as to form decorative puffs.
W – 11in(28cm); D – 10.25in (26cm), excluding net border.

94

Still in the 1780s, the Hampshire Museums collection holds an apron signed and dated 1787, shown in Plates II.77. This is a further example of a design including a border pattern, a corner motif and a scatter of tiny leaves over the ground. The border even includes filled cartouches, showing the tenaciousness of the earlier interest in intricate embroidery even near the end of the 18th century. The apron and neck ruffle shown in Plate IV.46, p167 are worked with the same border design, though the stitches and corner motifs differ. Aprons continued to be worn into the 1790s but, as we saw in Plate II.22, they became shorter and narrower and few survive. Kerchiefs also continued in use as shown by the fashion illustration in Plate II.78 but shawls and mantles with long flowing ends that could drape gracefully over the neo-classical dress of the period were particularly popular. Examples of both accessories are shown in the following Plates.

Plate II.77 (right) *Corner of an apron worked by Elisabeth Grimston aged 17 in 1787 (Hampshire Museums) This demonstrates that the knowledge and use of filling stitches was not totally lost in the late 18th century. Although the design includes cartouches, these are spaced apart rather than forming part of a continuous pattern and the corner sprays are completely detached from the border. Most of the lines are tamboured.*

Plate II.77a (left) *Detail of the apron in Plate II.77 showing the working of the inscription 'Elisabeth Grimston aged 17 1787'. The butterfly beneath it is the only one on the apron. The edge of the apron is worked with a row of holes like ladder stitch but with a tamboured line on the inside and buttonhole stitches on the outside.*

Plate II.78 (above left) Fashion plate showing two ladies in neo-classical robes of the late 1790s (courtesy of the Harris Museum and Art Gallery, Preston).

The lady on the left wears a kerchief with a pattern of discrete sprigs in the border and a larger sprig at the corner while the bottom of her skirt is decorated with stars, or flower heads, and dots: all these motifs could be embroidered. Dots and minute sprigs were so common at the time, sometimes covering whole dresses, that they are said to have given rise to the phrase 'going dotty' in reference to the poor workers who made a living embroidering them.

Plate II.79 (above right) Fashion plate of 1795 from the Hampshire Museum collections showing a lady wearing a cape-like garment with long ends. She also carries a fan and a bag, or reticule, which would have served a similar purpose to the work bags already discussed.

Plate II.80 *Detail of a handkerchief; c1790s. Although not identical to the kerchief in Plate II.78, this kerchief has a similar corner sprig and a border including dots and stars like that of the robe in Plate II.78. It is a complete square and is embroidered in the 'turn-over' fashion; that is, one triangular half is embroidered on one side of the fabric while the other is embroidered on the opposite side so that, when the kerchief is folded as shown, the right sides of the two corners are uppermost. Moreover, only the two corners intended to be displayed on the wearer's back carry the sprig design: the embroidery does not extend right into the other corners which are folded in wear. The embroidery is mainly in padded satin stitch which was becoming more common by this date and gives a greater contrast with the ground than many earlier stitches.*

1791 BOSWELL'S LIFE OF JOHNSON

1791-2 THOMAS PAINE'S 'THE RIGHTS OF MAN'

1793 EXECUTION OF LOUIS XVI

1796 JENNER'S FIRST COW-POX VACCINATION
AGAINST SMALL POX

1798 NELSON WINS BATTLE OF THE NILE

1799 NAPOLEON MADE FIRST CONSUL OF FRANCE

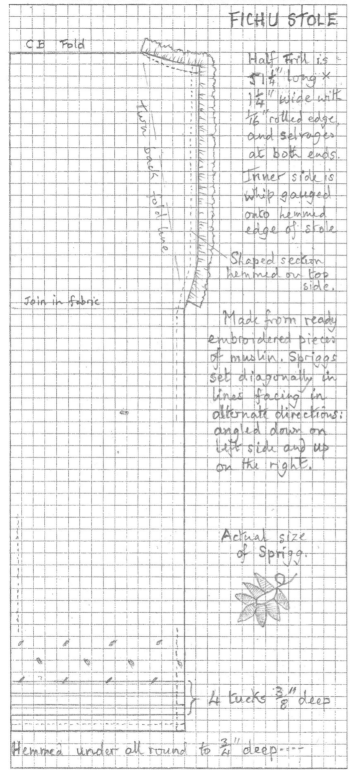

FICHU STOLE

CB Fold

Half Frill is 51¼" long × 1¼" wide with ⅟₁₆" rolled edge, and selvages at both ends.

Inner side is whip gauged onto hemmed edge of stole

Shaped section hemmed on top side.

Made from ready embroidered pieces of muslin. Sprigs set diagonally in lines facing in alternate directions; angled down on left side and up on the right.

Join in fabric

turn back fold line

Actual size of Sprigg.

} 4 tucks ⅜" deep

Hemmed under all round to ¾" deep---

Plate II.81 (left) *Pattern for a long shawl with an added gathered frill; c 1790s (Accession No. L 2359, Cavalcade of Costume, Blandford Forum). Scale of 1/8in = 1in.*

Plate II.81a (below) *Detail of the long shawl in Plate II.81. The frill extends along the central part of one side and along a notch cut so that the frill can be turned back. The entire article, apart from the frill, is embroidered with a regular array of tiny flower heads, typical of decoration from the 1780s to the 1810s. Kerchiefs and long garments with frills are frequently seen in costume plates from the 1780s and 1790s.*

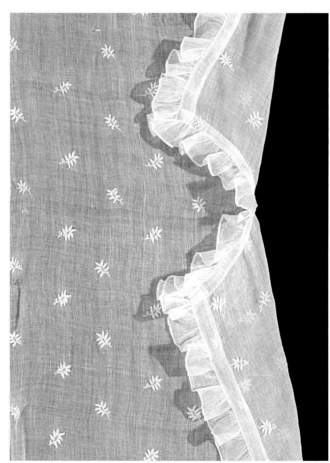

Plate II.81b (right) Detail of one of the end panels of the shawl in Plate II.81 showing the sprigged decoration and several decorative tucks.

Although we have now reached the end of our journey through the 18th century, we must return briefly to the 1780s to see yet another strand of design that was current at that time and had survived since the early decades of the century. We have already seen three designs from The Lady's Magazine of 1785 (Plates I.4, II.72 and II.75) but the volume further includes an embroidery pattern for a gown (Plate II.82) which could equally well have been employed for an apron. The pattern is far from classical in inspiration: it clings to the rococo with its scrolling C- and S-shaped stems. When seen in use, like that on the apron in Plates II.83, what comes to mind is the tree-of-life designs of the first quarter of the 18th century. As in those early designs, the branching stem pattern is repeated in the four quarters of the field, the upper repeats here lacking their uppermost stems. Only the extreme fineness of the stems, which are reduced to single lines, and the minuteness of flowers and leaves distinguish this design from its earlier counterparts. It should not be thought, however, that this design suddenly reappeared in the 1780s. Other examples can be found which have designs on scales between those of the 1720s and 1780s and which no doubt date from the middle decades of the century.

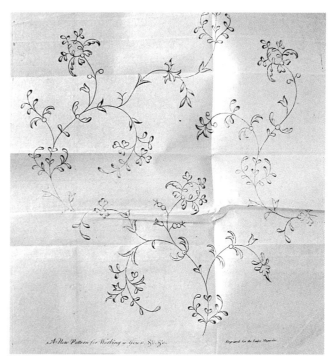

Plate II.82 Embroidery design for a gown from 'The Lady's Magazine' of 1785.
Like the design in Plate II.72, this design could easily have been worked by most amateurs either by needle-running or tambouring. Muslin or lawn would have been the fabric of choice whether the embroidery was to be in white or coloured thread: white was becoming more popular even for gowns by this date. The design would have to have been scaled up before use.

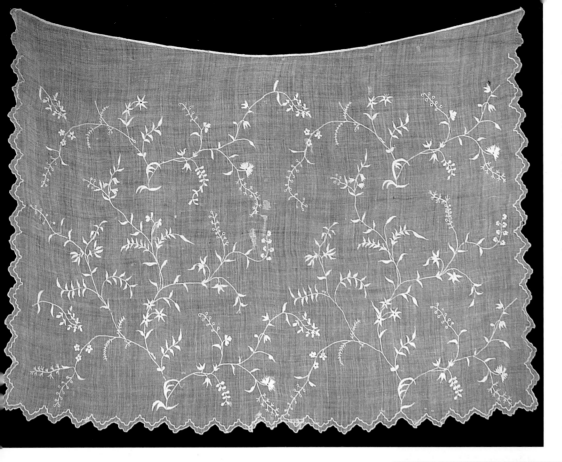

This brings our chronology of semi-transparent whiteworks for the 18th century to a close but, for part of the period, rather different forms of whitework were also in vogue for sturdier articles than ruffles, kerchiefs and aprons. These were items, such as waistcoats and stomachers, that were worn against the body and could not rely on the transparency of their ground for effect. These will be explored in SECTION III but, first, a few more words about the trade in whiteworked accessories and the fabrics from which they were made.

Plate II.83 (above) *Apron with two repeats of a trailing, leafy stem design below and two partial repeats above: the repeats are probably unfinished as the design would have been hidden when the apron was gathered onto a waistband.*

The main stems are tamboured while the side shoots are needle-run in a finer thread. Leaves and petals are worked in whipped running stitch with buttonholed eyelets at the flower centres: eyelets also form rows of seeds along some stems. The outer, dentate edge and the running line inside it are worked in buttonhole stitch.
W - 50 in (127cm); Ls - 35in (89cm): Lc – 32in (81cm).

Plate II.83a (right) *Detail of the apron in Plate II.83.*

MANUFACTURE AND TRADE

We have seen something of the manufacture of whiteworked costume accessories in the 18th century but little so far of how the raw materials were handled and the finished articles traded. The primary supplies were cotton and linen. Some flax for the linen threads was grown and processed in the British Isles, particularly in Ireland and Scotland, but the finest linens were imported from the Low Countries. Most cotton, on the other hand, was imported through our East India trade from the Middle East and, in particular, from India, until the latter part of the century when the Americas started to make an impact.

At the turn of the 17th-18th century, Indian printed cottons were so popular that it was made illegal to wear them in Britain to protect our home silk and woollen industries★. The trade in white muslins, however, continued to grow. Our workers also span and wove the imported materials (both raw cotton and thread) but, at that stage, our products were no match for the finest soft, translucent Indian muslins. With the Industrial Revolution, the picture was to change.

By the 1750s Kay's flying shuttle, first used in the 1730s for the manufacture of woollen broadcloth, was in use on cotton looms. One man could now operate a loom instead of two. The number of looms increased but there were too few spinners for the thread needed. At that time production was a cottage industry with the whole family involved: the children cleaned the raw cotton of seeds and dirt ready for the women who span the thread for their menfolk but, as three spinners were needed to supply one loom, additional thread often had to be bought in, if available.

Developed in the 1760s, James Hargreaves' 'spinning jenny' enabled one person to spin as much cotton thread as was spun initially by eight hand spinners, later up to one hundred. The machine was soon pirated and in widespread use: the bottleneck in production was broken but the jenny produced a lightly-spun, weak thread suitable only as the weft. Arkwright's 'water frame', set up in a water-powered mill built at Cromford in Derbyshire in 1771, produced a stronger thread, usable as a warp but suitable only for coarser fabrics such as calico. Then, in 1779, Crompton combined features of the Hargreaves and Arkwright devices to produce his 'mule' which produced a strong warp, as fine as those needed for the most diaphanous muslins.

These major inventions were accompanied by others for mechanising all stages of the conversion of fibre to yarn, including powering the various mechanisms first by water, then, from 1789, by steam, and improvements in bleaching and dyeing. There were setbacks as skilled workers saw their former livelihoods disappearing and rioted or broke machinery but, despite these problems, from the later 1770s onwards, Arkwright himself and other entrepreneurs built numerous powered spinning mills both in Lancashire and in Scotland.

In 1774, largely as result of Arkwright's lobbying, the ban on the wearing of printed cottons was lifted. Whereas in 1700, 1,000,000lbs of raw cotton were being imported, by 1764 this had risen to just under 4,000,000 lbs but by 1800 it was 56,000,000lbs. By 1785 British muslin was cheaper than Indian and it was said that women of all ranks, from the highest to the lowest, were clothed from head to toe in British-manufactured cotton.

By this time the American War of Independence was over. Liverpool had gained in importance as a port for the import of goods from the Americas including cotton from Brazil and the West Indies and, with immediate access to the Lancashire mills, was in prime position to receive the increasing trade from North America: there the East-coast cotton plantations had started production and British mills soon found the American supply more reliable than that from India under British rule. Here our tax system and method of collection gave farmers no incentive to ensure that the raw product they sold was in good, clean condition and of uniform standard.

In fact the wearing of imported printed cottons was banned in 1701, the ban being extended to our own prints in 1721.

Plate II.84 *Illustration from a supplement to Diderot's Encyclopedia showing the shop of a 'Marchand des Modes' which sold a wide range of made-up accessories (Courtesy of Bristol University Library).*

As the 18th century progressed, supplies of muslin became more plentiful but how were they marketed? Even when manufacture was a cottage industry, the weavers were not truly independent. Most received raw materials from a dealer to whom they subsequently sold the finished cloth, this system continuing with the machine-spun yarn. The wholesale dealers often had some outlets in the local retail trade but the majority of cloth was sold on to London warehouses or merchants. From here it was distributed to retailers in London, the provinces and abroad, with the export market becoming an increasingly important part of the trade.

As for the retail trade, numerous letters, accounts and other documents have been unearthed over the years that give us a general picture. For the basic fabrics, people could resort to the numerous linen drapers in towns throughout the country. These sold linens, cottons and mixed-fibre fabrics for everything from household use to dress although, for the finest fabrics, it was always necessary to resort to the London shops. The better drapers also kept some made-up accessories but, for finer and/or embroidered accessories, there were the haberdashers and milliners. The former sold a wide range of goods, very similar to what we might expect to find today, from fabrics to trimmings, including needles, threads, ribbons, buttons, wadding, binding, laces and some made-up articles but, generally, in the lower price ranges. An advertisement for the auction of stock from a London haberdasher included 'plain and flowered satins for cloaks and hats, plain strip'd and flower'd gauzes, various laces, hose, gloves, ivory fans, ribbons, chip hats, beads, threads, pins, needles, many other articles in Haberdashery way'. The entry for 'Haberdasher' in 'The London Tradesman, 1747', however, was very short and suggested that haberdashers needed no great skill, only a wide knowledge of prices as they bought from the wholesalers and sold at a moderate profit. Milliners were more specialist, selling more expensive fabrics, finer trimmings and accessories.

The entry under 'Milliner' in 'The London Tradesman, 1747' states that *'A milliner must be a neat needle-woman in all its branches and a perfect connoisseur of dress and fashion. She imports new ideas from Paris every post….. The most noted keep an agent in Paris to watch fashions and procure intelligence….. They have vast profits on every article they deal in, yet give but poor mean wages to every person they employ under them: though a young woman can work neatly in all manner of needle work, yet she cannot earn more than five or six shillings a week, out of which she is to find herself in board and lodging.'*

The entry also gives a list of goods traded in but the following stock list is more interesting as it includes prices: this is taken from the papers in bankruptcy of Elizabeth Brown, a Norwich milliner who had customers in the city, from the surrounding country and even London★. Among her stock, which included fabric for furnishing & clothing, trimmings, caps, hats, bonnets, shirts, stays, stockings, gloves, handkerchiefs and aprons, were: *'4yd clear lawn (woven with linen from which all roughness removed) £1; 2 clear lawn handkerchiefs 2s 8d; 1yd sprigged do 6s; Box of sundry muslin & lawn aprons & caps £2 2s; Box - a pair of treble ruffles, 1 pr double do & 1 handkerchief 14s 6d; 1 flowrd lawn apron 1s'.*

Despite the supposed difference between haberdashers and milliners, in reality the two trades overlapped. In 1766, for example, William Cart, Hatter and Haberdasher from Leicester, advertised his *'large and elegant Assortment of silks, muslins, caps, cloaks, aprons, handkerchiefs, gloves, trimmings and fashion jewellery as good an article and on good terms as any Warehouse in London'*★★. Yet more specialist were the lace dealers, most of whom had premises in London and of which there were two types: those who dealt in gold and silver thread laces and braids, made with real bullion, who also included the most exquisite embroideries in silk and metal threads among their wares: and those who dealt mainly in the linen laces and fine whiteworks, including Dresden work. The former had their own workrooms and/or put their work out to professional embroideresses. The latter bought in goods from the Continent and also from the dealers from the English lace-making areas who collected lace from their professional workers and brought it to London on a weekly basis: naturally some firms had representatives both in London and the provinces. Although all towns had their suppliers of more day-to-day wares and major provincial cities, like Bristol and Bath, had their specialist shops with high-priced goods, undoubtedly the best shops in England were in London. For those unable to go there, mail order was a possibility but many had purchases made for them by friends and relatives when they were in Town. Travelling salesmen might also call at the big houses as well as at local stores and markets. Altogether, there was plenty of choice and many women then, as now, loved shopping for clothes. Among numerous entries for clothing in the accounts of Elizabeth Jervis of Meaford in Staffordshire are the following relating to kerchiefs, aprons and ruffles:

1749 for a Gauze Cap Doub Ruffles Tucker & Ribin 17s6d;
1750 a Gauze handkerchief 2s6d;
1753 Dresden handkerchief £2.12s;
1756 Fishooe 7s6d;
1753 one pair of fine Dresden ruffles £1.15s;
1753 India pocket handkerchief 4s;
1769 14yds flowered cotton for two gowns £1.11s;
1753 Mrs. Rushton silk for foshu;
1755 black Lace for Foshoe 5s4d;
1757 lace for Foshoe 4s8d;
1769 Muslain for two handkerchiefs 7s3d;
1752 Cam(bric) for pr of ruffles 2s6d;
1753 Silisia lawn for Morning Ruffles 4s6d;
1748 Striped Muslain for Ruffles 4s6d;
1765 Muslain for Apron 12s;
1766 fine Muslain for Apron yd half wide & yd and full nail long 14s10d;
1750 Mininet Lawn for Kittys Apron a gift from me 16s10d;

★ *from 'A Provincial Milliner's Shop in 1785' by Pamela Clabburn in 'Costume', No.11.*
★★ *from the facsimile of Barbara Johnson's diary held by the V&A and published under the title 'A Lady of Fashion: Barbara Johnson's Album of Styles and Fabrics'*

1747 Scotts lawn for my girles aprons 9s9d;
1749 pd for yd & half of Muslain for Mr Jervis: Ruffles 13s6d'★.
('Fishooe/ foshoo' etc are clearly misspellings of 'fichu' but as this was not in common use in English in the 18th century one wonders how, if at all, they differed from 'handkerchiefs' which are also listed. The term is associated with the words 'silk' and 'lace' so it might have denoted a more expensive accessory than one of cotton or linen).
In these records, a clear distinction is made between articles that are 'ready-to-wear', such as the 'gauze handkerchief' bought in 1750, and fabric bought by the yard for making up, such as the cambric bought in 1752 for making into ruffles, although it must be remembered that, in 18th-century records, an entry for a 'gown' or 'robe' often meant the fabric rather than the made-up garment.
Patterned and plain fabrics are also distinguished: the cotton bought in 1769 for two gowns was 'flowered', i.e. decorated, usually but not necessarily with a floral pattern. At that time the ban on wearing printed cottons was in force so the pattern may have been tamboured (tambouring was very popular by that time) or woven, like that of the handkerchief in Plate II.60. The entries 'Dresden handkerchief' and 'fine Dresden ruffles' in 1753, however, can only mean articles with fine embroidery of Dresden type. Notably, the Dresden ruffles cost £1.15s, nearly eight times the cost (4s6d) of striped muslin for ruffles in 1748, and the Dresden handkerchief cost £2.12s, about seven times the cost (7s3d) of plain Muslain for two handkerchiefs in 1769. The difference represents the incredible amount of time and skill involved in the embroidery work.
In addition to payments for fabrics and accessories, Elizabeth's accounts include many payments for making garments and for cleaning, mending and altering but none for making aprons, handkerchiefs or ruffles or for embroidery. Presumably the fabrics bought for these accessories would have been made up by Elizabeth herself or a member of her household but they could have been put out to professional seamstresses either directly or through the fabric supplier. It is clear, for example, from

'The London Tradesman' that milliners employed sewers to make up accessories: the larger establishments had such employees on their premises but there were many independent seamstresses who took in what work they could as sewing was one of the few tasks a woman could do at home to support herself or contribute to a family income. George Thomson, for example, in 1744:
'Pd Mrs. Marriot making ruffled shirts @ 3s6d a piece £1 1s 6 do without ruffles @ 2s 6d 15s' and, in 1745, he paid
'Mrs. Dixon for making 12 shirts at 3s a shirt £1 16s New wristbands 2s 3d'
On 27 February 1747 he also bought **'a pair of Dresden Ruffles £3 3s'**★★. A single pair of embroidered Dresden ruffles thus cost nearly twenty times more than the making of a single ruffled shirt. They also cost about twice as much as Elizabeth Jervis's ruffles in 1753: assuming Mr. Thompson's ruffles were for shirt cuffs (it is difficult to think of an alternative) they must have been very fine as, although I have studied no surviving examples, men's ruffles as shown in portraiture are usually narrower than women's. As with all the fabrics and accessories priced in documents, there is rarely any way of comparing relative qualities.

★*'Records of the clothing expenditure for the years 1746-79 kept by Elizabeth Jervis of Meaford in Staffordshire' by Peter Hayden in 'Costume' No. 22/1988.*

★★*Taken from the facsimile of Barbara Johnson's diary held by the V&A and published under the title 'A Lady of Fashion: Barbara Johnson's Album of Styles and Fabrics': the diary was written in George Thompson's old account book.*

Another interesting inventory that gives some idea of the quantity of accessories used by an individual is that of Mary Churchill, 2nd Duchess of Montagu'★. In 1747, at age fifty-eight, Mary Churchill owned '35 prs sleeve ruffles (single, double & treble - lawn, cambric, muslin, fine lace, flowered &/or with lace); 47 handkerchiefs (— lawn, muslin, white flowered, gauze with silver lace); 38 aprons (18 of muslin, 2 of 'lewn', 7 of silk, 12 of Holland, including many described as 'striped', 'flowered', 'sprigged', 'finely worked'), 5 white cambrick pocket handkerchiefs, 7 laced handkerchiefs, 1 handkerchief all lace, laced ruffles, '4 pair of Ruffles - Brussels lace 2 pair of 'em are Cross-barr'd muslin'(diaper?), a plain single lappit head, laced tuckers, tuckers all lace, lawn & cambric tuckers , 3 pair of flourished muslin ruffles (2 pr single, 1double)'.

Once bought, fine whiteworked accessories needed a great deal of care to keep them in good order. In particular, ruffles needed to be removed from clothing for special attention then reattached: they and other articles could be sent out to specialist laundresses for washing, starching and pressing. Worn or torn items were carefully darned: some of the darns one finds are as beautifully worked as the original embroidery. Eventually the plain centres might wear out in which case the embroidery might be cut out and sewn onto new fabric. Specialists were also available for this task as shown by Mrs. Richardson's advertisement in the York Chronicle and Weekly Advertiser of 1772:

'Mrs. Richardson..... grafts old Dresden on new muslin so as not to be perceived where done'. Such 'grafting' could also update articles as fashions changed: the embroidery of the kerchief in Plate II.50 has been remounted on a larger triangle of muslin, presumably to suit the late 18th century fashion for buffons.

We have now considered the production and purchase of fabric and accessories and have seen various amateur embroideries in previous chapters but still know little of the British professional embroideress. 'The London Tradesman, 1747' has already been mentioned in relation to haberdashers and milliners: it lists all the major London trades at that time but 'Embroiderers' are listed only under suppliers to the lace-men who dealt in bullion laces. Here the concern was clearly with those working in coloured silks and metal threads: there is no mention of the embroideress in white threads on a white ground.

Various records could be cited of sewing and embroidery being taught in schools but there is little to indicate whether the children so taught continued to embroider for a living. Other records, particularly of apprenticeships, show that embroidery was regarded as a skilled craft and training might take seven years but the concern was particularly with standards of draftsmanship, the elegant use of colour and shading and placing of motifs.

Yet milliners, haberdashers, lacemen and the like sold embroidered muslins. Presumably some of the milliner's staff would have included whitework embroidery among the 'all manner of needle work' for which they could not 'earn more than five or six shillings a week' but the prizes offered in the 1750s for imitations of Dresden work drew few entries. We did not have sufficient highly-skilled specialists in whitework to supply our market in competition with the Dresden workers of Saxony. Certainly, until the Scottish industry, which will be discussed below, was set up in the 1780s, we had no concentrated body of workers devoted to one particular skill like those in Saxony or our lace-workers in Devon and the East Midlands.

Most of our professionals will, I fear, remain anonymous. One exception is the Moravian brotherhood. Members of this religious sect, which had its origins in Moravia and Bohemia, settled in England and by the mid 18th century had communities in various places. They had a strong work ethic: they believed in self-sufficiency, always working to a high standard but charging reasonable prices as they had no interest in riches, and they also believed in keeping records.

★ Taken from 'Inventory of her Grace's Things, 1747 — the Dress Inventory of Mary Churchill, 2nd Duchess of Montagu' by S. Llewellwyn in 'Costume' No. 31/1997.

Many of their menfolk were weavers and their women span and sewed and, in at least one community in 1770, the single sisters took up embroidery. They produced high-quality, fashionable goods, many of which were traded through the London market, their warden travelling to Town every week to deliver orders to certain shops and to take new samples of the sisters' work to obtain further orders. In addition, they had their own marketing outlets and received visitors to their communities, some of whom then became patrons. More importantly for their local townships, they also set up local schools and took apprentices from outside their own, closed communities★. The Moravians operated from communities scattered through the British Isles, including Ireland, but were a minority group and could not have had a major impact on the market. The same cannot be said of the Scottish industry. The west coast area had long been a centre for weaving when Scottish businessmen learned of the new cotton-spinning mills in the south. The first mills were built in the 1770s and by the 1780s many more were supplying the burgeoning market with fine white muslins required for the neo-classical style of dress.

Once the basic production had been established, manufacturers realised that value could be added to the plain product by embroidery. This was not entirely their own idea: an Italian, Luigi Ruffini, had set up an embroidery school in Edinburgh in 1782 in an endeavour to start an embroidery industry there and soon concentrated on whitework★★. His efforts were unsuccessful in the long term but provided the inspiration needed by the Glasgow manufacturers. The simple linear embroidery designs popular at the time could be effected very quickly in tambour work and embroidery workshops soon arose, particularly in neighbouring Ayrshire but also further afield in Scotland. In these workshops several women could sit on either side of long frames to tambour whole webs of muslin for sale not only in the UK but also to continental Europe. These women soon became known as 'the flowerers' (pronounced 'floorers') from the delicate, floral patterns they were accustomed to work.

A book of designs suitable for tambour work was published in Edinburgh in 1779 while the Royal Museum of Scotland in Edinburgh houses an early 19th century sampler from Old Cunnock, Ayrshire, which includes several tamboured designs of leafy swags and floral sprays suitable for arranging in the manner of the swags in Plates II.70 and II.71 but treated more delicately. The one point that many Glasgow manufacturers understood, and the lack of which spoiled many English products, was that for goods to sell in a competitive, fashion-conscious market they had to be well designed. Fortunately training in design for the decorative arts was provided in the Edinburgh School of Design and later in Glasgow and the Glasgow merchants made good use of the graduates. For some years, thousands of girls and women earned a better living at tambour work, even with pay rates as low as 1s 3d to 2s a week, than they could by their previous employment as spinners or domestic servants: in the same period, a skilled weaver might earn 7s a week.

Despite such a promising start the Scottish cotton industry suffered various setbacks in the 1790s and early 1800s due to the Napoleonic wars which disrupted both markets and supplies of raw materials. By the 1810s the flowing linear designs of tambour work were no longer fashionable and the embroidery side of the industry was in sharp decline. A new impetus was needed and came in the form of an entirely different style of embroidery, a style that was to become known as 'Ayrshire work', but here we enter a new realm which must wait for another book.

★ *Much more detail of the Moravian whitework industry can be found in Joslyn Baker's MA thesis on the subject in the Southampton University Library, Winchester campus - see 'Bibliography', p176 - and at the Fulneck Moravian Museum, Leeds*
★★ *Further details of Ruffini's career and of the Ayrshire cotton/embroidery industry can be found in Margaret Swain's various works - see 'Bibliography', p176.*

Section III

OPAQUE FORMS OF WHITEWORK IN 18TH-CENTURY COSTUME

The embroideries seen in the preceding chapters are worked on single layers of white muslin or fine linen and rely for their effect on slight differences in density between the semi-transparent ground, openings created by the needlework and denser areas of stitching or appliqué work. They are essentially two-dimensional works: there is little attempt to depict realistic, three-dimensional objects and only occasional couched-thread work, stitching in thick threads or padded satin stitch towards the end of the century create raised, three-dimensional surface work.

The next forms of embroidery to be considered are, at least in the latter respect, very different. One is quilting, in its various forms, which relies on the play of light on its raised, curved surfaces for its very subtle effects: the other employs a variety of surface stitches to create different textures which catch and reflect the light in different ways. Both forms of work may be combined in a single piece and, although they are used in circumstances in which the embroidered fabric is backed and/or worn close against the body, they may also include eyelet holes and drawn-thread work.

MEN'S WAISTCOATS

Many 18th-century portraits show gentlemen wearing lace ruffles down the front openings of their shirts and at their wrists and surviving accounts show that these might, alternatively, be of Dresden work but I can show no surviving examples. What do, however, survive are whiteworked waistcoats. Such an essential feature of 18th-century menswear as the waistcoat cannot be considered an 'accessory' but examples show such exquisite alternatives to the embroideries seen so far that they cannot be ignored.

A study of trade records from tailors' workshops, household inventories etc. demonstrates that plain white waistcoats in linen, cotton or mixed-fibre fabrics were widely used in the 18th century, often by servants, but there are few mentions of whiteworked examples. Some were certainly worked in Saxony alongside 'Dresden work'; others were amateur work including, no doubt, an example dated 1744 in the V&A collection ★. There are, however, few such dated examples nor any illustrations of them in wear: only the more expensive white silk waistcoats appear in portraiture. Our only guides to dating surviving examples, therefore, come from comparisons of the embroidery designs with other designs of the period and a knowledge of the changing shapes of men's garments through the 18th century. Many waistcoats have, however, been altered making shape a precarious reference.

There is thus insufficient evidence to provide rules for the close dating of surviving examples. In general, however, it appears that most whiteworked waistcoats date from the early-to-middle decades of the century when they were in vogue for informal, particularly summer wear. Most were embroidered to shape before the pieces were cut and made up into the garment like the waistcoat fronts shown in the embroidery workshop in Plate I.2.

As there is no room here for a large number of illustrations, a few examples must suffice to show the varying forms of embroidery used in their decoration. The cord-quilting displayed by the stomacher in Plate III.7 was also used on waistcoats.

★ See Hart, A & North, S, Historical fashion in Detail: the 17th and 18th Centuries, V&A, 1998, pp28-29.

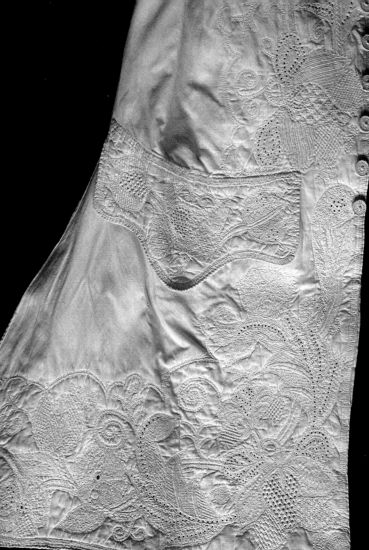

Waistcoat No.1

Plate III.1a Detail of the bottom part of a front panel of Waistcoat No.1 including a pocket flap and several of its 14 Dorset buttons. The quilting is worked through two layers of linen fabric, a finer outer layer and coarser inner layer, with soft wadding between them. There is no pattern repeat but some motifs are repeated in slightly different arrangements.

The motifs are intensely filled with stitching but set off against unworked areas of fabric which are puckered due to the quilting.

Plate III.1 Drawing of Waistcoat No.1 which can be dated to about the 1730s from the almost straight cut of the front edges of its front panels and the general style and scale of the design with its large, stylised motifs and variety of stitching.

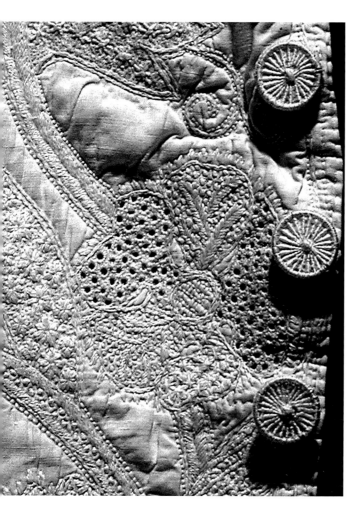

Plate III.1b *Detail of Waistcoat No.1 showing the Dorset buttons. Chain stitch, stem stitch and back stitch are among stitches used for lines in the design: oversewn eyelets feature widely in the fillings.*

Plate III.1c *A further detail of Waistcoat No.1 showing the density of stitching of the pattern motifs and the finishing of the edge.*

Waistcoat No.2

Accession No. - Cost No.184, Harris Museum & Art Gallery, Preston

Plate III.2 Waistcoat No.2; possibly made in the 1740s-50s from slightly earlier embroidery worked for a different purpose as the embroidery does not follow the shape of the front panels in the usual manner. The waistcoat is of linen twill with a finer lining; the embroidery is worked through the outer layer only and occupies a wide band down each front panel with a very narrow band of a different design across the bottom. The flow of the main design and large scale of the main motifs which are filled with smaller motifs and/or fillings suggest a date of about 1720-40 for the embroidery.

Front panel: max. length – 38.25in (98.5 cm); bottom edge – 13in (33cm) 1/2 chest: armhole to front edge – 11.5in (29.2cm); side slit to front edge – 10in (25.5cm); 24 Dorset buttons/buttonholes.

Plate III.2a (left) *Detail of Waistcoat No.2 showing: heavily raised outlines of couched threads; satin stitch; seeding; and counted-thread and drawn- or pulled-thread fillings.*

Plate III.2b (below) *A further detail of Waistcoat No.2 showing Dorset buttons worked over solid, probably wooden, forms and an edge finished with a line of stem stitching.*

Waistcoat No.3
An off-white silk waistcoat embroidered with self-coloured silk.

Plate III.3 (left)
Waistcoat No.3.
The embroidery design and stitching of this waistcoat are of fine quality but simpler and more repetitive than those of other waistcoats illustrated here. The construction and finish indicate that it was tailor-made. Its shape suggests a date of about 1740-60 which is consistent with the scale of the design.

Plate III.3a (opposite page left) *Detail of Waistcoat No.3. Satin stitch and French knots are the only stitches used.*

Plate III.3b (opposite page right) *Pattern for Waistcoat No.3. (Pattern scale 1/8in = 1in).*

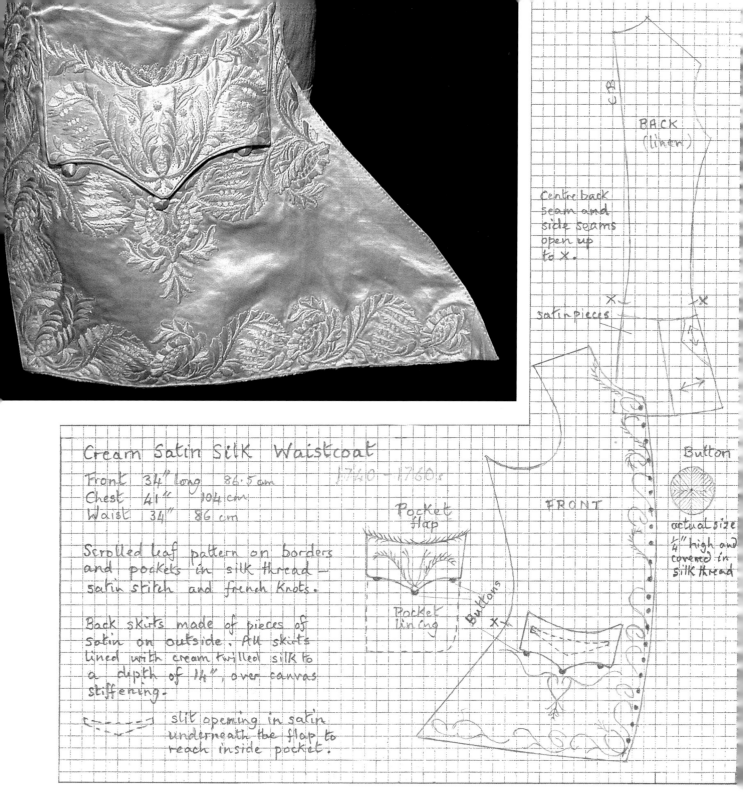

Cream Satin Silk Waistcoat

1740 - 1760s

Front 34" long 86.5 cm
Chest 41" 104 cm
Waist 34" 86 cm

Scrolled leaf pattern on borders and pockets in silk thread — satin stitch and french knots.

Back skirts made of pieces of satin on outside. All skirts lined with cream twilled silk to a depth of 14", over canvas stiffening.

- - - - - slit opening in satin underneath the flap to reach inside pocket.

BACK (linen)

C.B

Centre back seam and side seams open up to X.

satin pieces

X   X

Pocket Flap

Pocket lining

Buttons

FRONT

Button

actual size
¼" high and covered in silk thread

X

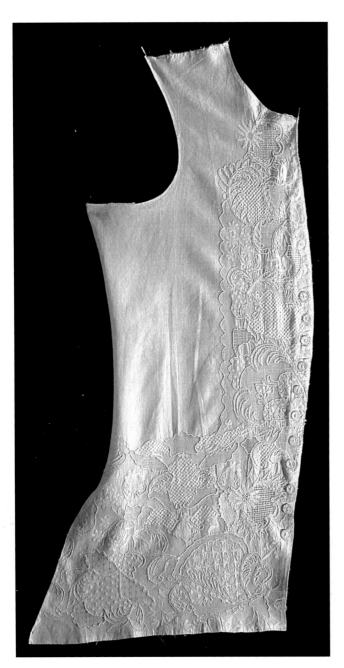

Waistcoat No.4
(Waistcoat front – altered from its original shape).

Plate III.4 Waistcoat No. 4 (opposite page left)
The embroidery is worked through only one layer; most of the lining is missing.

The scale and style of the embroidery design suggest a date of about the 1730s but the waistcoat has been recut at a later date. The work is very much lighter than in other waistcoats illustrated here and includes substantial areas of drawn-thread work. This is not, however, as intricate as the drawn-thread work used on fine muslins and forms larger openings which are more appropriate for use on a fabric which was backed in use. The fillings are worked symmetrically on the two halves of the waistcoat.

Front panel: max length – 32in (81.5cm); chest – 13in (33cm); bottom edge 14.25in (36cm) Depth of embroidery at bottom – 10.5in (27cm); front border 5.5in (14cm).

Plate III.4a (opposite page right) Detail of Waistcoat No.4. Most lines are in couched knotted threads but the flower stems are in chain stitch. Fillings include satin-stitch bricks, drawn-thread work and buttonholed rings. Flower petals and leaves are in buttonholed satin stitch.

'Knotting' was a favourite pastime of ladies in the 18th century: it occupied time gentilely and displayed elegant movements of the hands to any observers.

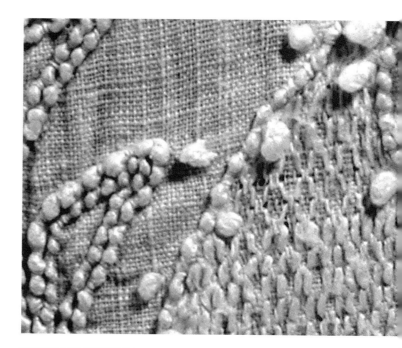

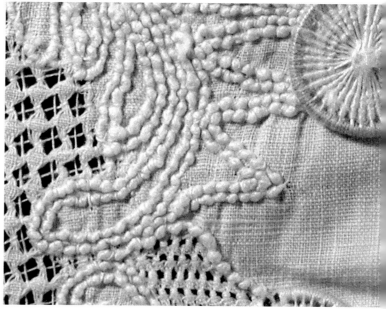

Plate III.4b (top right) Closer detail of Waistcoat No.4 showing a filling created by surface stitching.

Plate III.4c (bottom right) Further detail of Waistcoat No.4 showing the couched knotted thread used for lines in the design, two different drawn-thread fillings and a Dorset button. The couched knotted thread creates a lighter effect than the very closely oversewn threads used in the Harris Museum waistcoat – No.2.

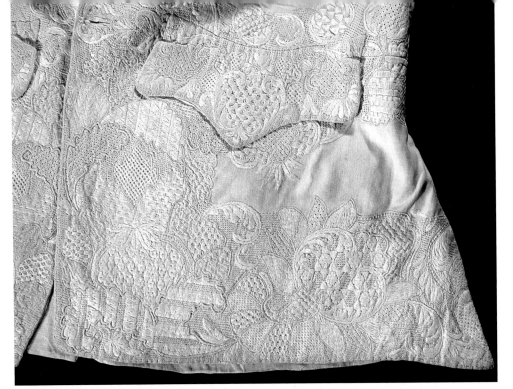

Waistcoat No.5
Accession No.1929-42,
Museum of Costume and
Textiles, Nottingham.

Plate III.5 *Lower part of an
altered waistcoat (No.5); the
front panels have been cut to a
new shape and the pocket flaps
have been moved.*
*The embroidery probably dates
from about 1720-40 and is
very similar in character to that
of the Harris Museum
waistcoat (No.2) except that,
whereas the Harris motifs are
embroidered against a plain
ground, here the ground itself
is embroidered. The work also
includes a wider variety of
surface filling stitches.*

Plate III.5a *Detail of
Waistcoat No.5.*

Waistcoat No.6

Plate III.6 *Drawing of a quilted waistcoat (No.6) bearing a label inscribed – 'Fine embroidered waistcoat, early 1700, belonged to an ancestor at one time an Alderman of Winchester; Mabel E. Roe': in fact it probably dates from the mid-18th century due to the cut-away shaping of the front panel and the general style of the design which is similar to that of mid-18th century Dresden works.*

Plate III.6a (above) *Detail of part of a front panel and pocket flap of Waistcoat No.6*

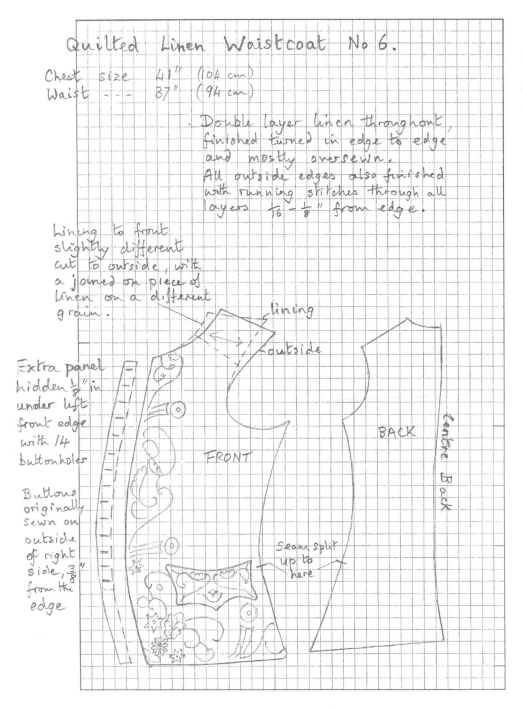

Quilted Linen Waistcoat No 6.

Chest size 41" (104 cm)
Waist --- 37" (94 cm)

Double layer linen throughout,
finished turned in edge to edge,
and mostly oversewn.
All outside edges also finished
with running stitches through all
layers $\frac{1}{16} - \frac{1}{8}$" from edge.

Lining to front
slightly different
cut to outside, with
a joined on piece of
Linen on a different
grain.

lining

outside

Extra panel
hidden $\frac{1}{2}$" in
under left
front edge
with 14
buttonholes

FRONT

BACK

Centre Back

Buttons
originally
sewn on
outside
of right
side, $\frac{3}{8}$"
from the
edge

Seam split
up to
here

Plate III.6b (left) *Pattern for Waistcoat No.6.(Pattern drawn on 1/8in squares to a scale of 1/8in = 1in)*

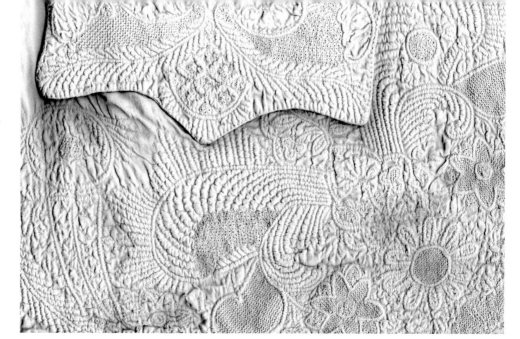

Plate III.6c *Further detail of the pocket flap and front panel of Waistcoat No.6.*
The quilting is worked in back stitch through two layers of linen fabric, a finer outer layer and coarser inner layer, with a soft wadding between them. The design has no pattern repeat but some motifs are repeated in slightly different arrangements. The fillings, including some drawn-thread work, are used symmetrically on the two halves of the front. The design covers almost the entirety of the embroidered area, there being practically no room for the plain ground between the motifs.
There are no surviving buttons but 14 buttonholes are hidden in a flap beneath the front edge of the left-hand front panel.

Plate III.6d *Closer detail of Waistcoat No.6 showing double rows of back stitches outlining main features of the design.*

WOMEN'S STOMACHERS

As we have seen when considering dress in the 18th century, the triangular gap between the edges of a woman's bodice was often filled by a stomacher which was pinned or otherwise fastened in place over the stays. Many surviving stomachers are elaborately decorated with coloured or metal-thread embroideries, lace or ribbons and were clearly intended for special occasions but a few whiteworked examples used for more informal wear also exist. These are decorated in a similar variety of styles to the whiteworked waistcoats but, as with the waistcoats, there are neither dated examples nor portraits to give a clear chronology.

A few examples are given here to demonstrate the variety of shape and design in use during the early to middle part of the century: a silk example has already been shown in plate II.64. The first example shows a form of quilting not so far illustrated but also used for waistcoats.

Stomacher No.1

Accession No.NG1033, Guildford Museum: first half of the 18th century.

Plate III.7 This stomacher displays a design of stylised flowers and leaves that is symmetrical about a vertical axis, a style that is common in stomachers. The scale and stylised nature of the motifs suggest a date in the early-mid 18th century. The work is 'cord-quilting', sometimes called 'Italian quilting', in which the raised effect is created by cords sandwiched between two layers of fabric, in this case a fine linen surface layer and a coarser backing. The casings for the cords are created by two lines of back stitching.

Stomacher No.2 (above)

Accession No.T224 1931, V&A: first half of the 18th century.

Plate III.8 This example is not strictly whitework as the design is cord-quilted in a pale blue thread but it could equally well have been worked in white. The ground is worked with white thread (not shown).
Centre front depth – 11.4in (29cm); Max. width – 8.75in (22.3cm).

Stomacher No.3 (below)

Accession No.Circ 3031911, V&A: about the second quarter of the 18th century.

Plate III.9 This stomacher is unusual in that, apart from the narrow band of decoration at the top, it has a large-scale asymmetric design. This, together with the stylised nature of the flowers and leaves, the oriental influence in the blossom at the bottom, and the wealth of filling stitches suggest that it dates from about the 1730s but the workmanship is not of high-quality professional standard and it may well be of later date.
The lines are created by couched threads and the fillings are all in surface work.
Centre front depth – 16in (40.6cm); Max. width – 12.5in (31.7cm).

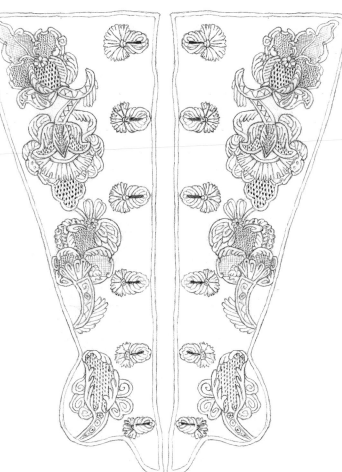

Stomacher No.5

(in two halves): Accession No.936.1897, V&A: probably about 1730-50.

Plate III.11 Although most stomachers were cut in single pieces, it is not rare to find them in two parts: one example has already been seen in Plate II.64. Here both parts have six buttonholes alongside their adjacent vertical edges that could be linked by pairs of decorative studs, ribbons or cords. The design of large, exotic blooms is quilted against a plain ground, with drawn-thread fillings worked through the two layers of fabric.

Centre front depth – 10.6in (26cm); half top width – 6in (15.2cm).

Stomacher No.4

Accession No.T209-1929, V&A: probably about 1730-50.

Plate III.10 Like Stomachers Nos.1 and 2, this example has a symmetrical design but the motifs are more crowded, on a larger scale and with motifs and intricate detailing in the rococo manner. The entire surface is quilted: linear parts of the design may incorporate cords while shaped motifs are created by softer wadding. Surface work, including seeding, is used for the fillings. Part of this stomacher is illustrated in 'Historical fashion in Detail: the 17th and 18th Centuries' by Avril Hart and Susan North.

Centre front depth – 13.75in (35cm); max. width – 11in (28cm); min width – 3.5in (9cm).

Stomacher No.6

Accession No.564.970.1,
Norfolk Museums and
Archaeology Service,
Carrow House Costume
and Textile Study Centre.

Plate III.12 The design of
this example is quilted partly
with soft cords, partly with
soft wadding which is placed
only where needed so as to
leave a plain, flat ground
between the motifs. The rococo
design suggests a date in the
mid-early second half of the
18th century.
The scalloped top edge is
finished with blanket stitch
which is not as well done as
the back stitch of the quilting.
Fillings are in drawn-thread
work.

Stomacher No.7
Accession No.M/C CAG 1947 1266; Manchester City Galleries.

Plate III.13 *The simple design of this stomacher is worked in cord quilting: each line of the drawing represents two back-stitched lines with the cord between them; probably second quarter of the 18th century.*

WOMEN'S POCKETS

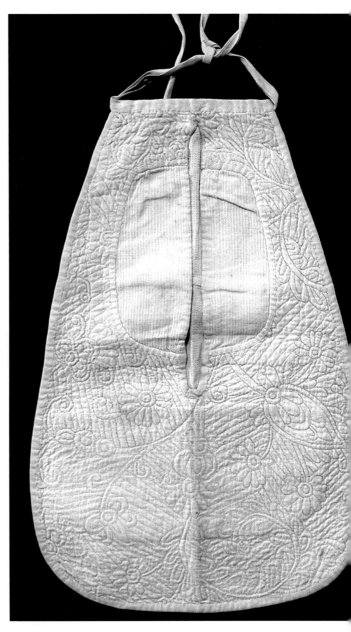

A feminine accessory mentioned only briefly so far is the pocket: in the 18th century pockets were separate items, usually worn in pairs attached to tapes which could be fastened round the waist with the pockets underneath the dress but accessible through side slits in the skirts. They were used to carry typical feminine accoutrements such as pocket handkerchiefs, vinaigrettes, pocket books and tools, fabrics and threads for various crafts which, in the later 18th century, might alternatively be carried in a work bag (see pages 93-4). Many surviving examples are beautifully embroidered: one wonders why when they were normally hidden beneath the skirts but a few portraits of ladies in domestic situations show the skirts hitched up to reveal the pockets, allowing readier access for the work in hand. As with the stomachers just considered, most surviving pockets are decorated with coloured embroidery although frequently this is cut from an earlier work.

Pocket No.1

Plate III.14 (opposite page right) One of a pair of quilted linen pockets with identical designs worked in backstitch in blue thread. The quilted fabric is cut from an earlier, larger piece and not designed specifically for the pocket. A piece of plain fabric is let in in the centre: the vertical slit through which access is gained to the pocket is cut through this. The backs of the pockets are of plain fabric, which is the norm. Max. depth - 13.25in (34cm); max. width - 9.25in (23.5cm); length of slit - 6.5in (16.5cm).

With the pockets are two notes: one, headed 'Nov 14 St Hilary, Cowbridge, South Wales', reads:
'Margaret Lady Tyler died in 1835 & is buried at St. Nicholas, also her husband Admiral Sir Charles Tyler K.C.B. They were the great grand parents of Lady Franklew and Col. Gerald Brues – the pockets were tied on under the dress skirt.'

The other, not in same hand, reads:
'These pockets belonged to my grandmother Margaret, Lady Tyler. This pillow case, I believe, was my sister's first cot pillow case March 1818. Emily Allen, St Hilary, Dec 29 1890'.

Plate III.14a Detail of Pocket No.1. The back stitch is worked through only two layers of fabric: there is no wadding between them.

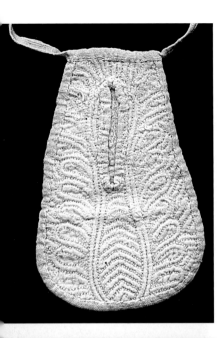

Pocket No.2

Plate III.15 (top left) Front of a miniature pocket probably made for a doll and cut from an earlier piece of cord-quilted linen.
D – 3.875in (10cm);
W – 2.625in (6.5cm).

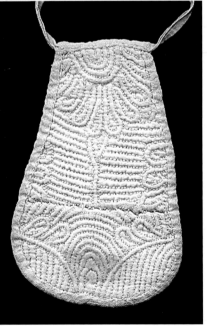

Plate III.15a (bottom left) Back of Pocket No.2.

Pocket No.3

Plate III.16 Drawing of a quilted linen pocket: Accession No.13065. Rachel B. Kay-Shuttleworth Collection Gawthorpe Hall. The quilted fabric is cut from an earlier, larger piece and not designed specifically for the pocket. The embroidery is worked in backstitch in yellow thread. The setting of a floral design against a vermicular ground was common in the early-mid 18th century.

Section IV

A SELECTION OF APRONS

Apron 1 (about 1730-60)

The quality and style of this apron mark it as true Dresden work. The border pattern includes repeats of three motifs, a large exotic flower head, a cartouche and a flower spray inside a narrow border of drawn-work. Dense pattern – shadow work. Lines – chain stitch; some double chain lines with lines of holes between. Edge – ladder-stitch with chain stitch on inside and blanket stitch on outside: top edge gathered into waistband.

W – 54in (137cm); Ls – 42in (107cm); Lc – 36.5in (107.5cm).

Plate IV.1 (below) Apron 1.

Plate IV.1a (right) Detail of Apron 1.

Plate IV.2 (above) Detail from one end of Apron 2.

Plate IV.2a (right) Detail from the centre of Apron 2 showing the join between the two fabric panels which differ slightly because of the hand spinning and weaving of the fabric. The embroidery is worked over the join.

Apron 2 (about 1740s) Norfolk Museums and Archaeology Service (Carrow House Costume and Textile Study Centre).

This extremely unusual, exuberant apron is made from two fabric widths. It has barley-twist pillars adjacent each end and in the centre with various mythical and comedia dell'arte figures and exotic birds in between. The pillars have acanthus leaves at top and bottom and flowers twining up them. The dating is suggested particularly by the domed shapes of some skirts but also by the birds which are much more freely drawn and lively than most of those in the 'tree-of-life' patterns in Plates II.26–II.30.

Plate IV.3 (above) Apron 3.

Apron 3 (about 1750-75)

This is unusual in having no border design but is
beautifully worked. The flowers in the large sprays are more
stylised, more Germanic than those in the apron in Plate
II.56. They are identical apart from mirror-imaging but are
interspersed with two different flower-basket designs.
Dense pattern – buttonholed satin stitch. Lines – chain
stitch; 2 parallel lines of chain stitch with dots between.
Edges – three rolled; top gathered and bound into 0.8cm
tape for 17.75in + 26.75in free ends. Other stitches –
buttonholed eyelets in flower centres.
W (1 fabric width) – 54in (137cm); Ls – 42in (107cm);
Lc – 36.5in (107.5cm).

Plates IV.3a & b (above) Details of 2 motifs from Apron 3.

130

Apron 4 (about 1730–60)

Accession No.1973.96, Nottingham Museum of Costume and Textiles.

Another fine example, probably true Dresden work. This item has been cut diagonally to form a kerchief but was originally an apron judging by the orientation of its central flower sprays. Although the border contains large cartouches and stylised flowers, the corner includes sprays of smaller flowers of a similar character to the sprays on the main field. Dense pattern – buttonholed satin stitch. Lines – chain stitch; some double chain lines with lines of holes between.

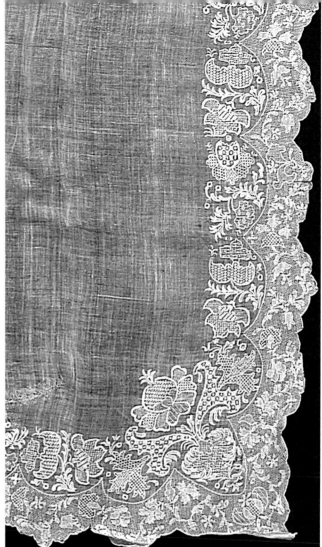

Plate IV.5 Detail of Apron 5.

Apron 5 (about 1730–60)

Accession No. TA 2607, Blaise Castle House Museum, Bristol. Another fine example, probably true Dresden work. Dense pattern – shadow work; buttonholed satin stitch. Lines – chain stitch (single and double lines). Edge – blanket stitch. W – 66in (168cm); Ls – 42in (107cm); Lc – 36.5in (107.5cm)

Plate IV.4 Corner of Apron 4.

Plate IV.6 Corner of Apron 6.

Apron 6 (about 1760-75)

This is tamboured throughout indicating a later date than suggested by the very bold, large scale of the border flowers. Edge – tamboured + bobbin lace; top edge altered. Pattern – large scale, exotic flowers with just over 2 repeats on each side; mirror imaged except for central variation on the bottom. 4 sprigs in grid formation in centre but not properly aligned; filling missing from 1 edge flower.
W - 42.5in (108cm); Ls -36in (91cm); Lc - 34in (86cm).

Apron 7 (about 1760-85)

An apron in the Exeter Museums collection (No. 50.1943.40) has the same border pattern with some identical fillings but used in different motifs: the sprigs scattered over the ground are slightly different. The asymmetric bell-shaped flower in the corner appears in a number of 18th century whiteworks. (See Plate IV.28b) Dense pattern and lines - tamboured. Edge – blanket stitch + bobbin lace with tamboured line just inside; top probably shortened as the embroidery goes over hem. Other stitches: drawn-thread fillings; tamboured eyelets. Border pattern - 2.25in (5.5cm) deep – 3 repeated large motifs on sinuous stems on plain ground;
W - 45in (115cm); Ls - 38in (96cm); Lc - 34.5 in (87cm).

Apron 8 (second half 18th century)

The boldness of the pattern suggests an earlier date than the sparseness of the design.

Dense pattern – buttonholed satin stitch. Lines – chain stitch (single and double lines). Sewn edge unclear – worked to form picots on a very narrow drawn-thread border; top edge pleated and bound with fabric – 16in (41cm). The border (2in/5cm deep) of small but dense alternating leaf and flower sprays gives a great contrast with the fine muslin. The centre has sprigs on a scale similar to those of Apron No.6 but more sparsely scattered. Very little filling work.

W – 51in (129cm); Ls – 37.5in (95cm); Lc – 34in(85cm).

Plate IV.7 (left) Corner of Apron 7.
Plate IV.7a (below left) Detail of Apron 7.
Plate IV.8 (below) Corner of Apron 8.

Apron 9 (about 1770–90)

Dense pattern – whipped running stitches. Lines – tamboured except for whipped running near edge. Edge – ladder stitch with buttonhole stitches on outside and chain stitch inside. Pattern; outer border of spaced cartouches with symmetrically arranged fillings with flowing pattern inside edge of fine flowering leafy stems tied with bows – just over 2 repeats on each side; powdering of sprigs over centre.

W – 58in (147cm); Ls – 34in (86cm); Lc – 33.5 in (85cm).

Plate IV.9 (top left) Corner of Apron 9.
Plate IV.9a (bottom left) Detail of Apron 9.

Plate IV.10 (opposite page, left) Detail of just over half Apron 10 showing the centre join and added upper panel.
Plate IV.10a (below) Closer detail of Apron 10.

Apron 10 (2 widths of fabric)

Dense pattern – satin stitch variation – worked as figure-of-8 through fabric. Lines - chain stitch. Edges – rolled except top edge. Pattern; 7 pairs of diagonal lines of leaf-like shapes with the same drawn filling (1 or 2 misplaced fillings); border pattern of festoons with different fillings not used symmetrically; embroidery worked over seams; very good and neat but odd mistakes suggest amateur work.

W - 76in (193cm) (2 fabric widths); Ls - 42in (107cm); Lc - 40in (101cm) deep increased from 37in (94cm) by extra fabric which also forms a binding along the upper edge.

Plate IV.11 (above) Corner of Apron 11.

Apron 11

This is worked in a much coarser thread than most other aprons. Dense pattern – whipped running. Stems - ladder stitch in larger sprigs; chain stitch. Edge – buttonhole stitch on outer edge + buttonholed line inside. Other stitches – buttonholed eyelets; very small areas of drawn work. Design – running border pattern along three sides with no centre of symmetry on the bottom: scatter of medium-size sprigs over centre.

W - 56.5in (143.5cm); Ls - 34in (86.4cm); Lc - 33.5in (85cm).

Plate IV.12 (below) pattern for the apron in Plate II.45, p65; and (right) pattern for the apron in Plate II.58, p79. (scale 1/8in = 1in).

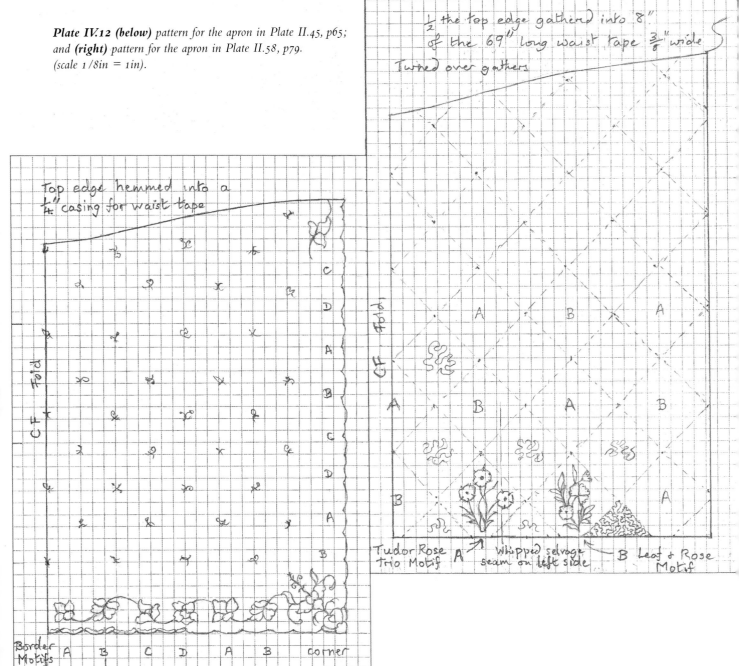

½ the top edge gathered into 8"
of the 69" long waist tape ⅜" wide
Turned over gathers

Top edge hemmed into a
¼" casing for waist tape

CF Fold

C
D
A
B
C
D
A
B

Border
Motifs A B C D A B corner

CF Fold

A B A

A B A B

B

A

Tudor Rose   A   Whipped selvage   B Leaf & Rose
Trio Motif   seam on left side   Motif

136

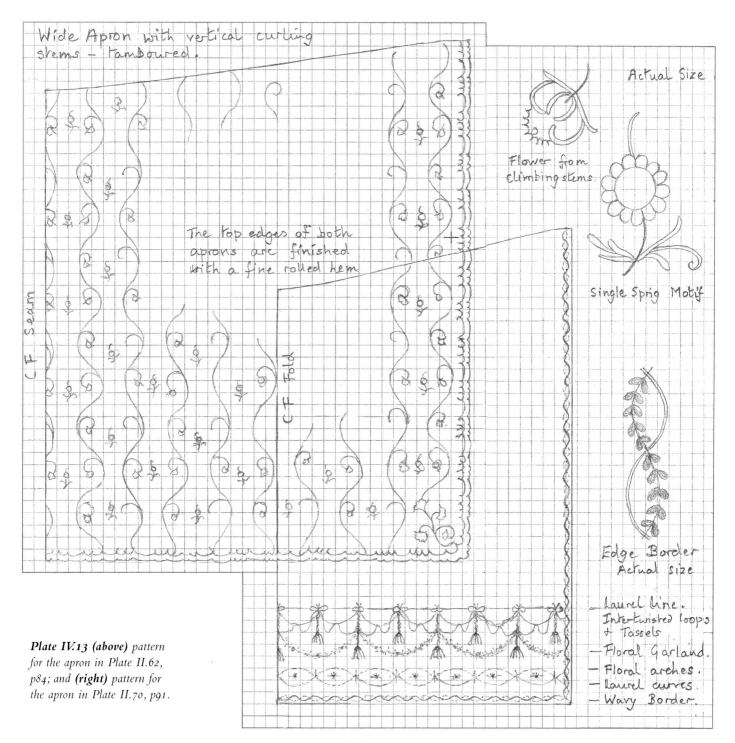

Wide Apron with vertical curling stems – tamboured.

Actual Size

Flower from climbing stems

Single Sprig Motif

The top edges of both aprons are finished with a fine rolled hem

C F Seam

C F Fold

Edge Border Actual size

– Laurel Line.
  Intertwisted loops + Tassels
– Floral Garland.
– Floral arches.
– Laurel curves.
– Wavy Border.

Plate IV.13 (above) pattern
for the apron in Plate II.62,
p84; and **(right)** pattern for
the apron in Plate II.70, p91.

137

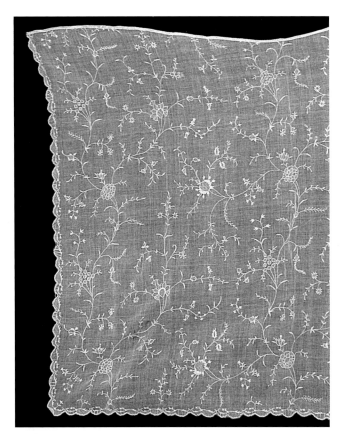

Plate IV.14 Detail of just over half Apron 12.

Apron 12 (about 1775-90)

This is tamboured throughout with drawn-thread fillings in the border cartouches. The all-over pattern has three repeats across the width and just over two down the length with slight adjustments at the edges and bottom to fit the design neatly within the space available. The pattern could alternatively repeat continuously for a dress fabric.

Apron 13 (ultra-fine muslin) (about 1780-95)

Pattern – running stitches throughout; double lines for stems. Edge – blanket stitch. Other stitches – large buttonholed eyelets and small overcast eyelets. Design – very narrow, simple border of separate leaves and flower heads; centre filled with 4 sinuous floral trails and 2 trails of trefoils extending down the length with separate sprigs between them.
W - 50in (127cm); Ls – 41.5in (105.5cm); Lc - 36.25in (92cm); top 16.75in pleated except for 1.75in at centre and bound into linen tape; (34in & 35in tape free); 2.5in fabric turned over at centre.

Plate IV.15 Apron 13.

Set I - matching apron and kerchief

This set is in fine Dresden work, with the same classic Dresden design, but the kerchief is in a slightly more closely-woven fabric than the apron.

Dense pattern – shadow stitch.

Stems – chain stitch; some double lines. Edges – buttonholed; kerchief neck edge rolled; apron top bound into 15.5in (39.5cm) tape +29in (73.5cm) extra for each tie.

Apron: W - 49.5in (128cm); Ls - 38in(96.5cm); Lc - 35in (89cm); border pattern - 3.25in (8.3cm); corner pattern - 7.75in (19.7cm). Kerchief: Ls - 29in/28.5in (73.5cm/72.5cm); CB - 10.75in (27.4cm).

Plate IV.16 (top) Lower part of apron and matching kerchief of Set 1.

Plate IV.16a (right) Details of apron and kerchief of Set 1. The kerchief is in a slightly denser fabric than the apron.

A SELECTION OF KERCHIEFS

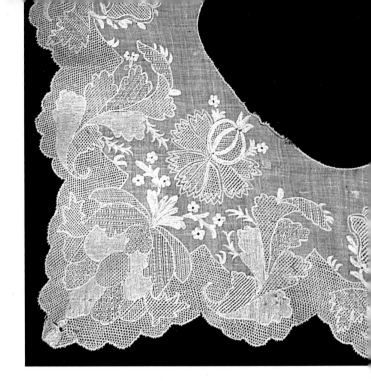

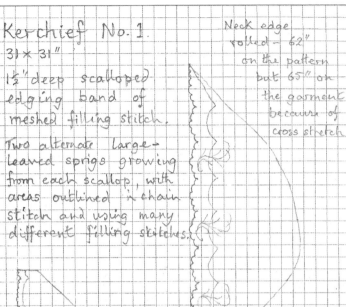

Kerchief No. 1.

31 × 31"

1½" deep scalloped edging band of meshed filling stitch.

Two alternate large-leaved sprigs growing from each scallop, with areas outlined in chain stitch and using many different filling stitches.

Neck edge rolled - 62" on the pattern but 65" on the garment because of cross stretch.

— Centre Back

Kerchief No. 2. 29" × 29"

Baroque style large floral design with multiple filling stitches, and shadow work. Outlines in chain stitch.

½" scalloped border of filling stitches, & small buttonholed scallops with a picot edging.

Plate IV.17 Patterns for Kerchief 1 and Kerchief 2.

Plate IV.18a (opposite page top) Detail of Kerchief 1.

Kerchief 1

This has an unusually wide outer border worked with the same ground filling throughout: 2 alternate motifs of large leaves and stylised floral sprays spring through this into a plain centre (3.5 repeats on each side). Fillings are used regularly but there is no great variety.

Dense pattern: larger areas – rows of blanket stitch worked alternately in opposite directions give a very light effect; leaves and small areas in buttonholed satin stitch. Lines – chain stitch. Edge – blanket stitch with needle-worked picots; neck edge rolled.

Ls – 30.75in (78cm);
CB – 9in (23cm);
D (border) – 4 in (10cm).

Plate IV. 18 (top right) Kerchief 1.

Plate IV.18b Close detail of Kerchief 1 showing the surface blanket stitching on the right which creates moderately dense pattern areas, small motifs in buttonholed satin stitch, the drawn-thread ground and fillings, and chain-stitch outlines.

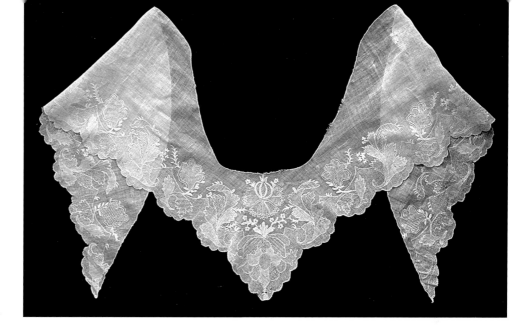

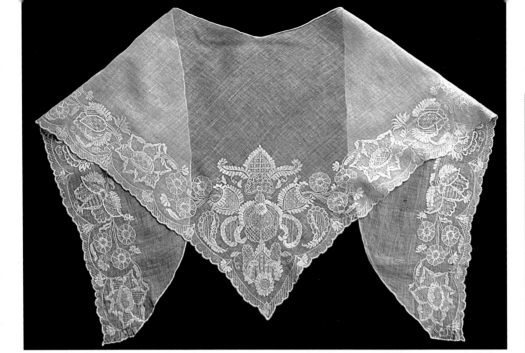

Kerchief 2 - Fine Dresden work

(See Plate IV.17 for Pattern) Dense pattern – shadow stitch; buttonholed satin stitch. Lines – chain stitch; some double lines. Edges – buttonholed + bobbin picots; neck edge rolled Each main border has 8 motifs with only the end ones repeated; the outer border has 2 alternating drawn fillings. Ls – 29.25in (74cm); CB - 16in (40.5cm); D (border) - 3in (7.5cm); D (corner) - 8.75in (22.5cm).

Plate IV.19 (opposite page top left) Kerchief 2.
Plate IV.19a (opposite page right) Border of Kerchief 2.
Plate IV.19b (opposite page bottom left) Detail of Kerchief 2.

Plate IV.20 (right) Corner of Kerchief 3.

Kerchief 3

Accession No.1883.8. Museum of Costume and Textiles, Nottingham. This shows yet another 18th century kerchief shape: it is L-shaped with tapered ends but the interesting feature is the central notch. Dense pattern – shadow work. Lines – chain stitch; shadow work. Edges – neck edge rolled. Ls – 33in (84cm); D of L-shape arms – 7in (17.8cm).

Plate IV.20a (right) Detail of Kerchief 3.

143

144

Plate IV.21a (above) Border of Kerchief 7.

Kerchief 4

Accession No. 1978.510, Museum of Costume and Textiles, Nottingham.
Dense pattern – buttonholed satin stitch; shadow stitch. Lines – chain stitch.
Ls – 29.5in (75cm); CB – 13.25in (33.7cm).

Kerchief 5

Accession No. T8220, Blaise Castle House Museum
Dense pattern – buttonholed satin stitch. Lines – chain stitch; whipped running; shadow stitch. Edge – blanket stitches inside a rolled hem; neck edge rolled.
Other stitches - blanket stitch wheels and overcast eyelets.
Ls - 31in (78.5cm); CB – 9.5in (24cm).

Plate IV.21 (opposite page) Clockwise from the top, corners of Kerchiefs 4, 5, 6, 7.

Kerchief 6

(half-handkerchief – see Plate IV.21 and Plate IV. 25 for detail)
Dense pattern – buttonholed satin stitch. Lines – chain stitch. Edge – blanket stitches outside narrow drawn border with 2 fillings alternating in scallops; neck edge rolled. Design – unusual complex arrangement of trailing stems carrying a variety of small, medium and large motifs, some fine, some clumsily drawn but well worked in fine thread; fillings are not as varied as in many works. The pattern repeats twice either side of the centre with a slight change at the ends. The plain centre has been replaced.
Ls - 32in (81cm); CB – 23in (58.5cm); border pattern – 5.5in (14cm) narrowing to ends; corner pattern – 8.25in (21cm).

Kerchief 7

Dense pattern – shadow work. Lines – chain stitch, mainly double and within motifs. Edge – neatly scalloped; blanket stitch; neck edge probably altered. Other stitches – very varied drawn fillings. Design - typical Dresden work and style; just over 2 pattern repeats on each side; fillings are repeated in the same motifs almost throughout.
Ls - 30in (76cm); border – 5in (12.7cm); corner pattern – 9.25in (23.5cm).

145

Plate IV.22 *Pattern for Kerchief 8 (left) and Kerchief 9 (right). (scale 1/8in = 1in).*

Kerchief No 9

33" × 32½"

84 cm × 82.5 cm

Plate IV.23a (above) *Close detail of Kerchief 8.*

Kerchief No 8   31" × 32"

Floral design with filling stitches and satin stitch

Inside edge on pattern 49", on garment 56".

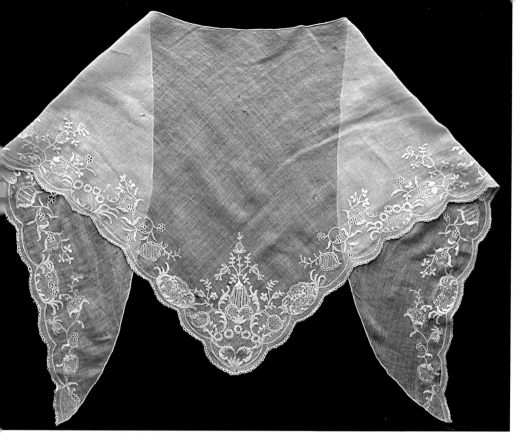

Kerchief 8 (See Plate IV.22 for Pattern).
The design is very light in character, with spreading stems and tiny leaves and flower heads, but still contains some large motifs and cartouches in every third scallop along the border: the sprays between cartouches are different but they and the drawn fillings are arranged symmetrically along the two sides.

Dense pattern – buttonholed satin stitch; satin stitch. Lines – tamboured chain stitch; ladders edged with chain stitch. Edge – shallow scallops edged with buttonholed rings worked on the fabric with chain stitch along inner edge + 3/8in band of drawn-work with the same stitch throughout; neck edge rolled. Other stitches – buttonholed eyelets – larger ones form little flowers; ladders between rows of blanket stitch. Ls – 31in/30.5n (76cm/79cm); CB – 17in (43cm); Corner pattern – 7in (18cm).

Plate IV.23 (above) Kerchief 8.

Plate IV.23b (right) Border of Kerchief 8.

147

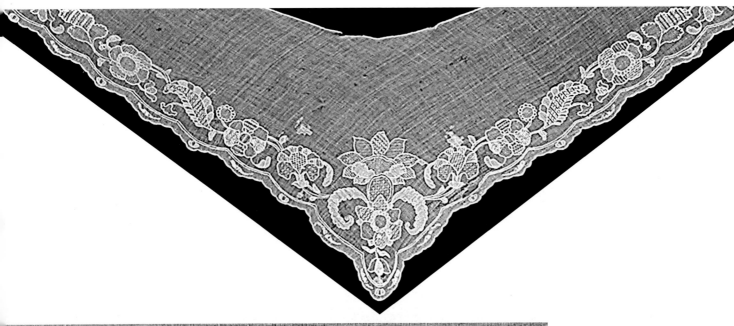

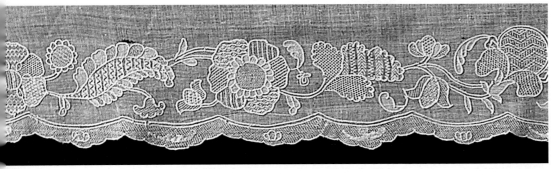

Kerchief 9 (See Plate IV.22 for Pattern).
The use of darning for the dense areas which are, in any case, very small makes this design very light despite the large scale of the motifs.
Dense pattern – darning.
Lines – chain stitch.
Edges – buttonholed; neck edge rolled.

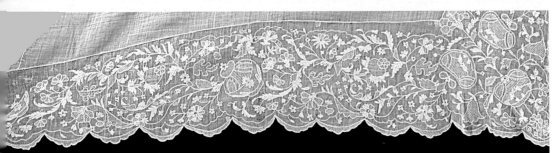

Plate IV.24 (top) Detail of Kerchief 9.
Plate IV.24a (above left) Border of Kerchief 9.

Plate IV.25 (left) Border of Kerchief 6 (Plate IV.21).

Plate IV.26 Corners of
Kerchiefs 10, 11 and 12.

Kerchief 10 (top – sprigged, late 18th century - see Plate
IV.27 for Pattern).
Dense pattern – tiny areas of buttonholed satin stitch. Lines
– chain stitch. Edge – worked to form picots; neck edge
rolled. Design: lozenges formed in the scalloped border
have 6 different drawn fillings worked in extremely fine
thread; their order varies slightly in the 16 scallops in each
border but they are mirror-
imaged on the two sides;
the main design of fine
sprigs in a diamond grid
formation is not
completely regular – there
are 56 motifs of several
different designs.

Kerchief 11 (centre - half-
handkerchief or buffon, 1790s-
early 1800s).
The repetitive border design
extends along only two sides
but the entire ground is
spotted. The neck edge is
rolled; the other two edges are
hemmed with a 2mm hem. All
edges curve slightly because of
the extreme fineness of the
fabric. All work is tamboured.
Ls – 38in (96.5cm);
CB – 32in (81cm));
border – 2.25in (5.7cm).

Kerchief 12 (right-half handkerchief or buffon, about
1790s - see Plate IV.27 for pattern).
This has only a narrow border design but it extends along
all three sides. The laurel trail intertwined with parallel
tamboured lines is classically inspired while the tiny
asymmetric sprig in the main corner has a rococo feel. It is
tamboured throughout except for the rolled edges held
with blanket stitch; a tamboured line runs inside the edge.

Plate IV.27

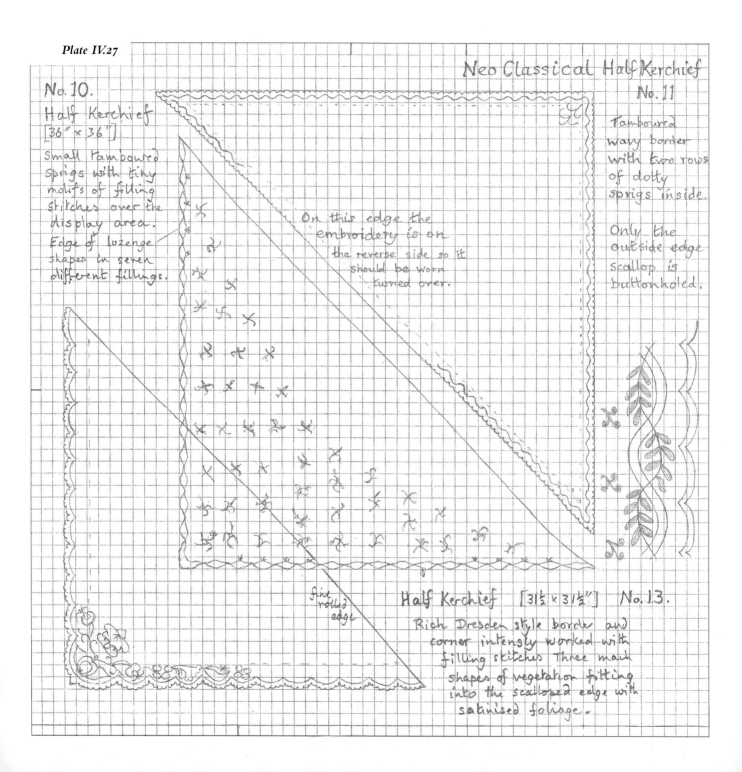

Neo Classical Half Kerchief

No. 10.

Half Kerchief
[36" x 36"]
Small tamboured sprigs with tiny motifs of filling stitches over the display area. Edge of lozenge shapes in seven different fillings.

No. 11

Tamboured wavy border with two rows of dotty sprigs inside.

Only the outside edge scallop is buttonholed.

On this edge the embroidery is on the reverse side so it should be worn turned over.

fine rolled edge

Half Kerchief [31½ x 31½"] No. 13.
Rich Dresden style border and corner intensely worked with filling stitches. Three main shapes of vegetation fitting into the scalloped edge with satinised foliage.

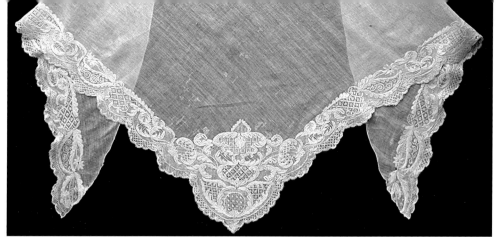

Plate IV.28 Kerchief 13.

Plate IV.28a Detail of the corner of Kerchief 13.

Plate IV.27 (opposite page) Pattern for Kerchief 13 (below), Kerchief 10 (centre) and Kerchief 12 (above). (Pattern scale of 1/8in = 1in).

Kerchief 13

(half-handkerchief – see Plate IV.27 for pattern) Dense pattern – buttonholed satin stitch; shadow work in outer border. Lines – varying widths of stem stitch; chain stitch, particularly inside 1/2in deep outer border. Edge – blanket stitch + bobbin picots. Design - great contrast between the dense border and sheer muslin centre; 3 pattern repeats of 3 different motifs on each side; the fillings are not quite the same in the repeats but are almost mirror-imaged on the 2 sides; 2 fillings alternate in the outer scalloped border. Ls – 31.5in (80cm); CB – 22in (56cm); corner pattern – 7in (18 cm); border – 2.25in (5.7cm).

Plate IV.28b Border of Kerchief 13 showing the 3 motifs of the pattern repeat.

Set 2: Matching kerchief and sleeve ruffle

(See Plate IV.32 for pattern of ruffle) The kerchief edging has been remounted on a larger triangle of muslin: the original design has been continued onto the new ends but the workmanship is much poorer than the original. The ruffle is unusual in that its decorated, free edge is straight, apart from the scallops, and its opposite edge, which is gathered in use, is shaped (see pattern). The simple, unexaggerated shape suggests that this set was made before ruffles expanded in the mid 1750s. Dense pattern – buttonholed satin stitch in original; darned in later extension. Lines – chain stitch; Edge – buttonholed. Ls (original) – 30in (76cm); (current) -34.5in (87.5cm); border – 2.5in (6.5cm)

Plate IV.29 Kerchief of Set 2.

Plate IV.29a Borders of Kerchief (above) and sleeve ruffle of Set 2 (below) showing the matching patterns and the extension of the kerchief border when the embroidery was remounted.

A SELECTION OF SLEEVE RUFFLES

Sleeve Ruffle 1

Single; muslin on later linen band. Dense pattern – tiny areas of buttonholed satin stitch. Lines – overcast thread of different thicknesses and stitch spacing (often 2 twist thread). Edge – inverted blanket stitch with picot tufts. Other stitches - multiple drawn fillings; overcast eyelets. Design – discrete floral and leafy sprays on a plain ground inside a 3/8in deep scalloped outer border of discrete motifs on a ground of very varied drawn work. L - 35in (89cm); D - 4.75-10in (12-25.5cm).

Plate IV.30 (top)
Sleeve Ruffle 1.

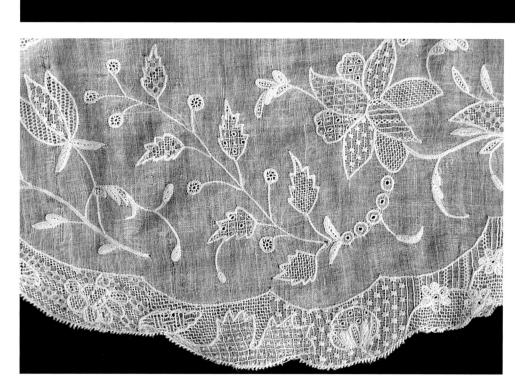

Plate IV.30a *Detail of Sleeve Ruffle 1.*

Sleeve Ruffle 2

(See Plate IV.32 for pattern).

Single, gathered to linen band. The design of this very fine Dresden-work ruffle is almost hidden in the drawn-thread ground but is similar in character to that of Ruffle 6 (p158). Its restrained shape and complex design suggest a mid 18th century date. Dense pattern – shadow stitch in narrow areas including stems.

Lines – running stitch; couched threads. Edge – overcast with picots.

Plate IV.31 *Sleeve Ruffle 2.*

Plate IV.32 (opposite)
Patterns for sleeve ruffles (scale of 1/8in = 1in).

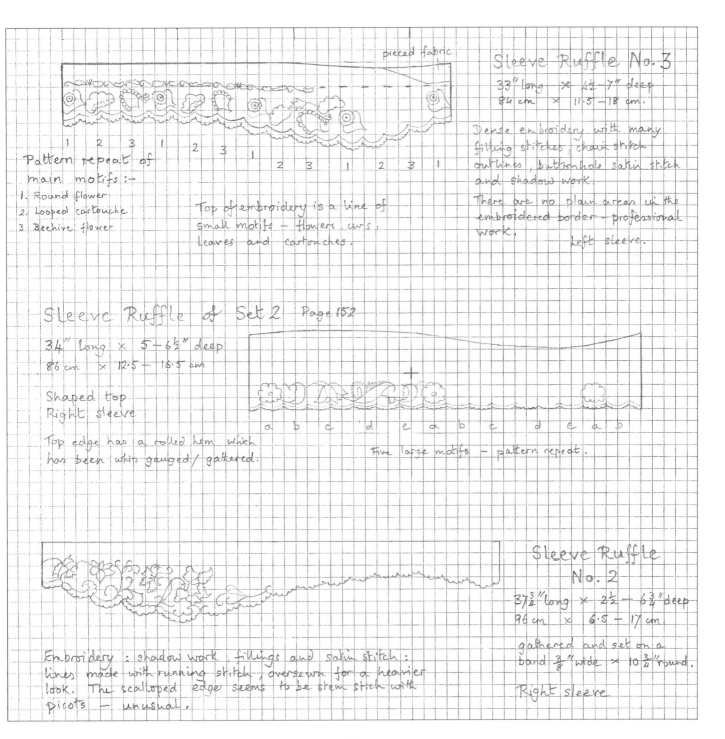

pieced fabric

33" long × 4½–7" deep
84 cm × 11·5 – 18 cm.

Pattern repeat of
main motifs :-
1. Round flower
2. Looped cartouche
3 Beehive flower

1 2 3 1 2 3 1 2 3 1

Top of embroidery is a line of
small motifs – flowers curls,
leaves and cartouches.

Dense embroidery with many
filling stitches, chain stitch
outlines, buttonhole satin stitch
and shadow work.

There are no plain areas in the
embroidered border – professional
work.
            Left sleeve.

Sleeve Ruffle of Set 2   Page 152

34" long × 5 – 6½" deep

86 cm × 12·5 – 16·5 cm

Shaped top
Right sleeve

Top edge has a rolled hem which
has been whip gauged / gathered.

a b c d e a b c d e a b

Five large motifs – pattern repeat.

Sleeve Ruffle
No. 2

37¾" long × 2½ – 6¾" deep
96 cm × 6·5 – 17 cm

gathered and set on a
band ⅜" wide × 10¾" round.

Right sleeve

Embroidery : shadow work, fillings and satin stitch:
lines made with running stitch, oversewn for a heavier
look. The scalloped edge seems to be stem stitch with
picots – unusual.

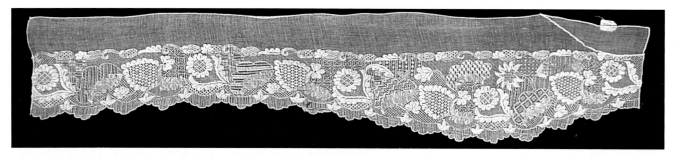

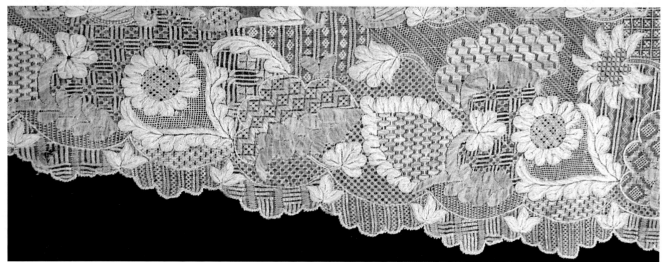

Plate IV.33 (top) Ruffle 3.
Plate IV.33a (bottom) Detail of Ruffle 3 showing the dense patterning.

Sleeve Ruffle 3 (See Plate IV.32 for pattern); mid 18th century.

Dense pattern - buttonholed satin stitch; shadow stitch. Lines - chain stitch. Design – the main pattern is confined between inner and outer borders and consists of closely-spaced but unconnected motifs set against a complex drawn ground with a variety of stitches; there is no flow to the design. Alternate scallops in the outer border are filled with two different stitches. Both ruffles of the pair are pieced, probably at a later date than the original embroidery.

Sleeve Ruffle 4

Accession No.CB1110/199325 Allhallows Museum, Honiton. Dense pattern – shadow work + surface stitching Lines - chain stitch. Edge – chain stitch + bobbin picots. Other stitches - overcast eyelets. Design – the unusually broad flowing stem in surface stitching carries very large stylised flowers, fruits and smaller sprays. The area between the stem and scalloped edge is filled with drawn work – the same stitch throughout.
L – 38.25in (97cm); D – 7.5 - 8.5in (19-21cm).

Sleeve Ruffle 5

Double Ruffle. This is tamboured except for the drawn fillings in the border. Edge – bobbin picots.

Plate IV.35 (top) Double Ruffle 5: the smaller of the two flounces of the double ruffle is folded and placed over the other which is incomplete.

Plate IV.35a (middle) Detail of one flounce of Ruffle 5.

Plate IV.34 (left) Detail of Ruffle 4.

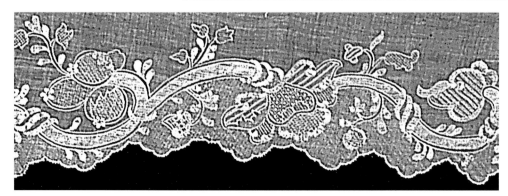

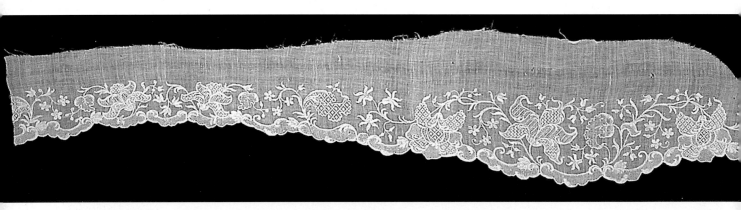

Sleeve Ruffle 6 in very fine Dresden work.
Dense pattern – shadow stitch in narrow areas including stems. Lines – chain stitch. Edge – buttonhole stitches over rolled edge. The border has the same drawn filling throughout except where large flowers cut though it but most of the floral design is set against a plain ground, making it easier to read than that of Ruffle 2.

L – 36.5in (93cm) (shortened); D – 7in (18.0cm) max but straight edge altered.

Plate IV.36 (top) Ruffle 6.
Plate IV.36a (above) Detail of Ruffle 6.

158

Sleeve Ruffle 7

Accession No. CB1171.2/2004 32.5 Allhallows Museum, Honiton.

This has a fairly unusual design with symmetry about an axis through the widest part of the ruffle. Dense pattern – buttonholed satin stitch; satin stitch. Lines - chain stitch; double running in finer thread. Edge – inverted blanket stitch with tufted picots. Other stitches – buttonholed eyelets and half eyelets. Design – the use of leaf and floral motifs to form frames for floral sprays, most of which **Plate**

IV.37a Detail of Ruffle 7.

spring from the outer border, is more typical of lace designs than whitework designs and suggests a date of about 1750-70; the 1/2in outer border contains a multitude of fillings with no symmetry whereas the fillings in the main pattern are used symmetrically.

L – 40.5in (103cm); D – 5-10in (12.7-25.5cm).

Plate IV.37 (bottom) Ruffle 7.

159

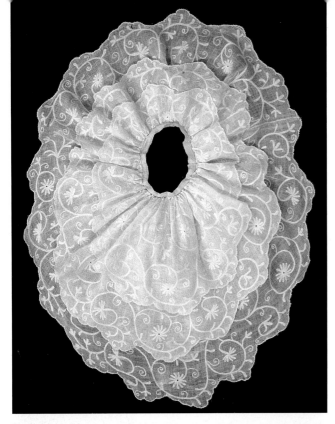

Sleeve Ruffle 8

Triple, muslin gathered to later silk ribbon; Accession No.11881, Rachel B. Kay-Shuttleworth Collection. Pattern- entirely tamboured. Edge – blanket stitch with thread used to make picots. Other stitches – eyelets in flower centres kept open with chain stitch. Design of scrolling stems and tendrils with tiny leaves and flowers covers the entirety of the narrowest, uppermost ruffle but only the outer portions of the other two.

Plate IV.38 (top) Triple Ruffle 8. © Rachel B. Kay-Shuttleworth collection.
Plate IV.38a (bottom) Detail of one layer of Triple Ruffle 8. © Rachel B. Kay-Shuttleworth collection.

Sleeve Ruffle 9

Double, muslin gathered to linen band. Dense pattern – darned, all in very fine thread. Lines – running stitch, mostly double. Other stitches – drawn fillings, little variety.
This is worked in very fine thread giving an airy feel to the design which flows continuously round the ruffles.

Plate IV.39 (opposite top left) Double Ruffle 9.
Plate IV.39a (opposite bottom left) Detail of Ruffle 9.

Sleeve Ruffle 10

Double; muslin gathered to linen band; Accession No.PH 186, Pickford House, Derby.
This is tamboured, with the same drawn filling used throughout the border which is finished with a bobbin picot edging. The strong, simple design worked in a very thick thread contrasts with the very light design of Ruffle 9 though they probably both date from the 1760s–80s.

Plate IV.40 (opposite top right) Double Ruffle 10; a few tiny sprigs are scattered over the ground.
Plate IV.40a (opposite bottom right) Detail of one layer of Double Ruffle 10.

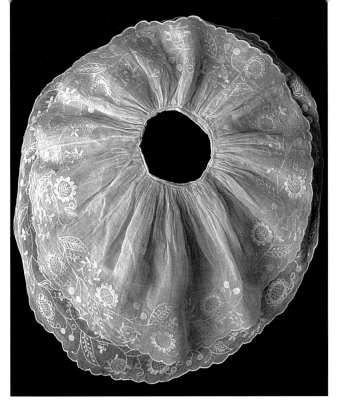

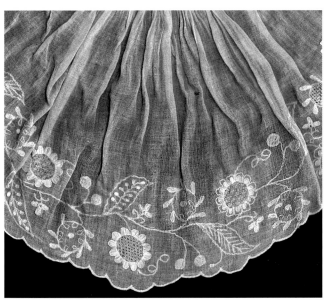
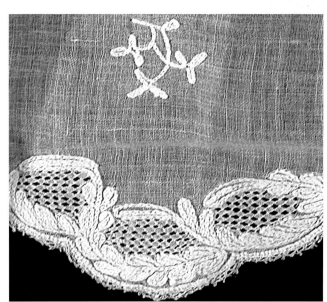

Sleeve Ruffle 11 (See Plate IV.42, for pattern).
Dense pattern – chain stitch – 2-3 lines only in tiny areas.
Lines – chain stitch. Edge – blanket stitch with picots
worked in embroidery thread. Other stitches – drawn
fillings; overcast eyelets. Design - the very narrow outer
border has a wide variety of drawn fillings; other fillings are
less varied; the sprays of large flowers on slender, curving
stems are carefully organised to finish on a line 3in in from
the straight edge of the ruffle.

Plate IV.41 (top) Ruffle 11.
Plate IV.41a (above right) Detail of Ruffle 11.
Plate IV.41b (above left) Closer detail of Ruffle 11.

Plate IV.42 (opposite page) Patterns for Ruffles 11, 12 and 13 in
order from top to bottom. (scale of 1/8in = 1in).

162

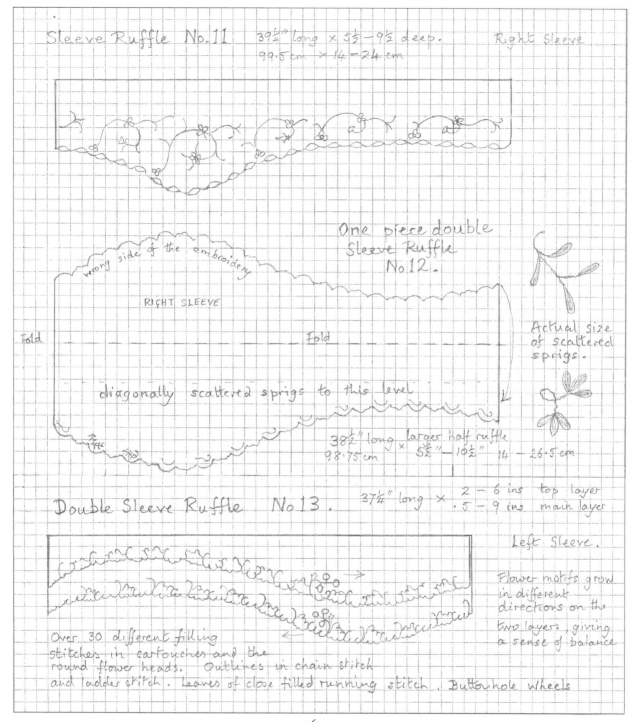

Sleeve Ruffle No.11   39½" long × 5½ — 9½ deep.   Right Sleeve

99.5 cm × 14 — 24 cm

One piece double
Sleeve Ruffle
No.12.

wrong side of the embroidery

RIGHT SLEEVE

Fold _____ Fold

Actual size
of scattered
sprigs.

diagonally scattered sprigs to this level

38½" long larges half ruffle
98.75 cm × 5½" — 10½" 14 — 26.5 cm

Double Sleeve Ruffle   No.13.   37¼" long ×   2 — 6 ins top layer
.5 — 9 ins main layer

Left Sleeve.

Flower motifs grow
in different
directions on the
two layers, giving
a sense of balance

Over 30 different filling
stitches in cartouches and the
round flower heads. Outlines in chain stitch
and ladder stitch. Leaves of close filled running stitch . Buttonhole Wheels

163

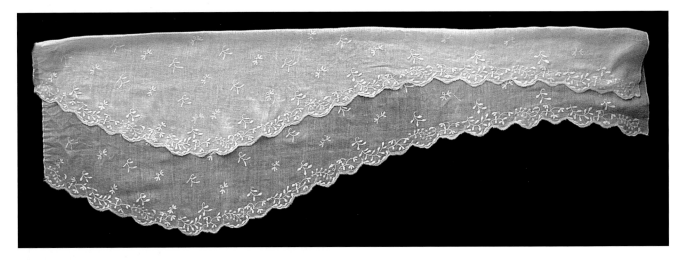

Sleeve Ruffle 12 Double ruffle (See Plate IV.42 for pattern).

This is the only example I have come across of a double ruffle of this type cut in one piece. Dense pattern – satin stitch in border sprays and 1 line of sprigs; running stitch in other sprigs. Lines – slanted stitches with 2 threads involved, probably worked in opposite directions. Edge – blanket stitch + bobbin picots. Other stitches – ladder stitch; overcast eyelets + back stitch giving star-like appearance.

L –38.5in (98cm); D – 3.7 – 5.25in (9.5 –13.3cm); wider – 8.75 – 11in (22.3 – 28cm).

Plate IV.43 (top) Double Ruffle 12 with the narrow ruffle folded over the wider one as in wear.
Plate IV.43a (left) Detail of the borders of Ruffle 12.

Plate IV.44 (opposite top) Double Ruffle 13: the narrow ruffle is placed over the wider one as in wear.
Plate IV.44a (opposite middle) Detail of the border design of the narrower flounce of Ruffle 13.
Plate IV.44b (opposite bottom) Closer detail of the wider flounce of Ruffle 13.

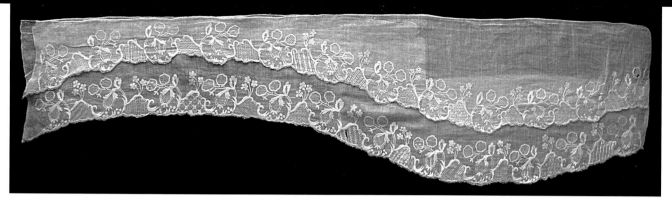

Sleeve Ruffle 13 Double, muslin (See Plate IV.42 for pattern).

Dense pattern – whipped running stitch. Lines – chain stitch; ladder stitch with chain stitch each side. Edge – blanket stitch + bobbin picots. Other stitches – drawn fillings; buttonholed eyelets. Design – although the designs in the two ruffles are the same, they are effectively mirror-imaged as the rock-like cartouches are the opposite way round and the floral sprays curve in opposite directions into the spaces between them.

L - 36in (91.5cm); D - 1.75- 6in (4.5-15cm); wider - 4.25 – 7in + 0.75in added band (10.8-17.8cm + 2cm); border about 2.25in (5.8cm)

(The wider ruffle has been increased by an extra band, 0.75in wide, probably in the original make-up).

Plate IV.45 *Engraving of Alan Ramsay's portrait of Lady Erskine showing her wearing a neck ruffle and hooded lace cape, both common items of wear in the 1750s–60s. (Courtesy Bristol University Library).*

MISCELLANEOUS ITEMS

This section includes several items of slightly uncertain purpose together with other items which do not fall into the main categories of aprons, kerchiefs and sleeve ruffles.

Set 3: Matching apron and neck ruffle

Neck ruffles, usually of lace in portraiture, were often worn from the 1750s through into the early 19th century and were part of the romantic interest in antique fashions throughout this period: they were inspired by the ruffs of the Elizabethan and Jacobean periods but never acquired their enormous proportions. This example is made up from a whiteworked border with the same design as the accompanying apron. The border design is, in fact, identical to that of the apron worked by Elisabeth Grimston in 1787 (Plate II.77) although the stitches and corner motifs used are different.

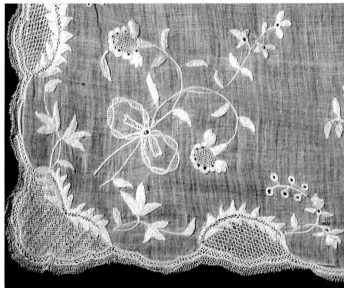

Plate IV.46a *Detail of the apron border. Dense areas are in buttonholed satin stitch, lines in chain stitch. The edges of both items are finished with a narrow bobbin lace with picots.*

Plate IV.46 Set 3: *apron and neck ruffle with the same border design; c1780s.*

Plate IV.46b *Pattern for the neck ruffle in Plate IV.46. (scale of 1/8in = 1in).*

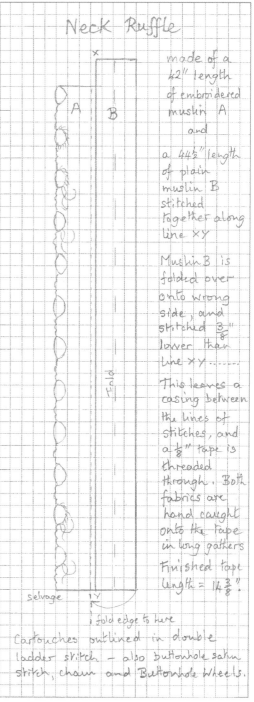

Neck Ruffle

made of a 42" length of embroidered muslin A

and

a 44½" length of plain muslin B stitched together along line XY

Muslin B is folded over onto wrong side, and stitched 3/8" lower than line XY......

This leaves a casing between the lines of stitches, and a ⅛" tape is threaded through. Both fabrics are hand caught onto the tape in long gathers

Finished tape length = 14 3/8"

A   B

Fold

selvage   Y

fold edge to here

Cartouches outlined in double ladder stitch — also buttonhole satin stitch, chain and Buttonhole Wheels.

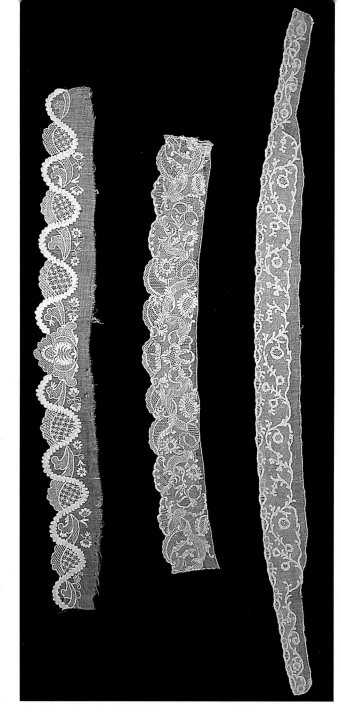

Borders with symmetrical designs

The next plate shows three borders with symmetrical designs, the right-hand one being reduced in depth at the ends. Although not shown here, each border is one of a pair. The symmetry of the designs of the central and left-hand borders makes one wonder how they were intended to be used: most borders worked in long lengths from which pieces are cut to form trimmings have repetitive designs. The two examples are of very different qualities: the embroidery of the left-hand example is simple and in fairly coarse thread whereas the central one is of the finest Dresden work.

One would be just as puzzled by the other border if it were not for the similarly-shaped ruffle shown with it in Plate 47b. The latter is one of a pair of ruffles of Mechlin bobbin lace which, like the whiteworked example, has different designs in the wider and narrower portions, but its ends are joined so that it forms a circular ruffle. The curious feature is that it is the edges of these ruffles that are gathered in wear that are shaped, not the free decorated edges as is usual.

Several examples of this type of ruffle are illustrated in the Dresden Catalogue where Dr. Bleckwenn dates them to between 1740 and 1790 according to their designs which are very varied. Some pairs are worked back-to-back on a single length of fabric but, since they do not appear to have been used, it is not certain that they would have been gathered to form a double ruffle for wear or cut apart and worn singly.

Plate IV.47 Three whiteworked borders with designs that are symmetrical about a central axis. The ends of the right-hand border, also seen in Plate 47b, are deliberately reduced in depth from the undecorated edge.

Left-hand border – 31.5in x 3.25in max. (80cm x 8.3cm). Central border – 26.25in x3.25in max. (66.5cm x 8.3cm). Right-hand border : L (overall) – 42in (107cm); L (wide part) – 28in (71cm); D max. – 2.75in (7cm): D min. – 1.5in (3.7cm).

Plate IV.47a (above) *Detail of the central border in Plate IV.47; c1750s. Dense areas are in shadow stitch, lines in chain stitch; the scalloped edge is buttonholed. The convolutions of the ribbon suggest a date in the third quarter of the 18th century for this border. The work is of exquisite delicacy: the drawn fillings are used symmetrically and even the ground is drawn.*

Plate IV.47b (right) *Detail of the right-hand border in Plate IV.47 together with one of a pair of Mechlin bobbin lace ruffles. The design of the Mechlin lace dates it to about the 1750s: the more open design of the whitework suggests a date in about the 1760s.*
Whitework border: dense areas - appliqué work with a corded outline: the entire ground is drawn; the edge is buttonholed. Mechlin ruffle: L (overall) – 38.5in (98cm); L (wide part) – 20.5in (52cm); D max. – 2.4in (6cm): D min. – 1.5in (3.8cm).

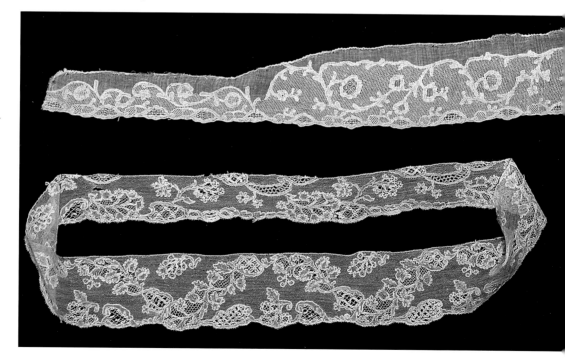

Joined lappets

The next uncertain item is a pair of lappets joined at about 90 degrees to each other by a roughly triangular corner piece. I have seen many 18th century lace lappets in this form but the original, separate lappets have been adapted to this use, often by being joined by part of the matching cap crown which has been cut up. The whitework lappet shown on the right in Plate II.36, which is joined to a second lappet through a similarly-embroidered square, has been adapted in this manner. It has generally been assumed that such adapted lappets were worn as a fichu or used to edge a kerchief and, indeed, some have had their inner edges cut off presumably for sewing to a triangle of fabric: others show no sign of sewing to another fabric. The whitework examples in Plates IV.49 are not adaptations: they were clearly made in this form originally. They fit quite neatly around the neck with the triangular point at the back like a kerchief. Alternatively they work quite well as a headdress with the point over the forehead and the lappets hanging behind. The illustration in Plate IV.48 shows both possibilities.

Plate IV.49 (opposite top) A pair of mid-18th century lappets in fine Dresden work made integrally with a centre piece. The fabric of one lappet includes a join but the embroidery is worked over it. The lappets have a scalloped edge all round finished with inverted blanket stitch and tufted picots; their designs flow beautifully from the centre down to the ends, fitting neatly within both scalloped edges. Was this accessory intended to be worn round the neck or on the head or perhaps adaptable for either use as occasion demanded? Ls – 28.5in (72.5cm); D (lappet) - 2.5in (6.3cm); D (corner) - 5.5in (14cm).

Plate IV.48 Drawing of a detail from the portrait of Lady Betty Germain by Phelps, 1731. Lady Betty is shown in court dress. She wears a cap which comes to a point over her forehead with lappets hanging behind but with no sign of the frill which usually frames the face: the edge of the cap crown appears to be continuous from the point at the front down to the end of the lappet. Lady Betty also wears a narrow band of fabric round her neck with the two ends crossed in front and tucked into the top of her stomacher. The fabric appears textured and may possibly be fur but demonstrates that narrow scarves were in fashion at the time.

Plate IV.49

A kerchief edging in fine
Dresden work: mid 18th century.
Although this is approximately the
same shape and size as the item above,
the long ends are designed as borders with
finished, scalloped edges on their outer sides and
undecorated edges along their inner sides (the inner
edges are rolled but may have been altered from the
original shape).
Ls − 31.5in (80cm); D (border) -3in (7.7cm); CB - 6.75in
(17.2cm). (See page 172 for details)

Another pair of
whiteworked lappets made
integrally with a centre piece;
Accession No.CB1170/ 2004.32.4,
Allhallows Museum, Honiton.
The design is neither typically English nor
German. The narrow border pattern extends right
round enclosing a space packed with large, simply
drawn motifs and fine tendrils.
Ls − 26.5in; D (lappet) - 2.5in (6.3cm); D (corner) - 5.5in
(14cm). (See page 172 for details)

Plate IV.50 (right) *Detail of the top item in Plate IV.49*
Dense areas are in buttonholed satin stitch in a loose, shiny thread;
lines in chain stitch; all other parts are decorated with drawn work.
(centre) *Detail of the central kerchief edging in Plate IV.49. The*
design of this border, with its very large stylised flower heads springing
from a patterned edge, is typical of one form of Dresden design.
Dense areas are in buttonholed satin stitch; the scalloped edge is
buttonholed; lines in chain stitch; the motifs contain fine drawn work
but the ground is plain.
(far left) *Detail of the bottom item in Plate IV.49*
Lines are in overcast threads; there is no dense work.
The three details are not to the same scale.

Plate IV.51 (below) *Closer detail of the top item in Plate IV.49.*

CLEANING, CARE AND CONSERVATION

The majority of items illustrated in this book are made of cotton and have been washed many times in the past but washing is an invasive technique that can weaken fibres and removes evidence of past history. Conservators are ever more wary of subjecting museum objects to washing or other forms of cleaning. Dirt left in fabrics can, however, cause wear or decomposition and looks very unsightly if the object is to be put on display. A choice needs to be made. If you are not familiar with handling old fabrics, you should consult a textile conservator but, if you do decide to do your own washing, here are some guidelines. Just remember, articles that may be over two hundred years old need far more gentle handling than they had while in use if they are to survive for future generations to enjoy.

Washing
Suitable for cotton and linen items.
1. Choose a suitable container for the process – if possible it should be big enough for the article to be washed to be laid flat. In the home the bath may be best for size and ease of draining but it must be washed and rinsed thoroughly before you start.
2. Place a sheet of melinex (Regd. TM) large enough to support the item in the container.
3. Lay the item as flat as possible and soak in cold water for about an hour then rinse thoroughly (if necessary it can be lifted out of the container on the melinex to facilitate changes of rinsing water).
4. Soak in a dilute, luke-warm solution of a mild, liquid detergent such as those sold for babies: if possible consult a conservator regarding current preferred detergents. DO NOT use general washing detergents that contain bleaches, biological agents, blue whiteners etc., all of which can harm old fabrics.
5. Use a clean sponge and press gently and repeatedly on the item, moving over its surface to force the detergent through it and help remove dirt: DO NOT rub.
6. Rinse extremely thoroughly to remove all signs of detergent and give one or two final rinses in deionised water (available from chemists).
7. Pat the item with clean towels to remove excess moisture; lift out of the container on the melinex if necessary and place on a flat support to dry naturally.

If this gentle treatment does not remove stains, seek professional advice. If it still looks grubby, a second treatment a few weeks later can be effective.

Silk Specialist dry-cleaning is safest, especially if the silk is lined with linen or cotton, which is often the case with 18th-century items.

Ironing
Only, if at all, on a cool setting.
After washing, some fabrics are soft and do not set into hard creases, in which case it is better not to iron them; others become more supple with a light steam – unfortunately only experience can say which treatment is better for any particular item. Any ironing should be done with a cool iron (heat is bad for old textiles) while the fabric is slightly damp. Any decorated parts should be placed face down on a towel and the item ironed on the wrong side so as not to flatten any raised work.

Storage
The aim should be to prevent creases, to keep out light, dust, insect pests and harmful chemicals, and to keep in a stable, cool environment.
Minimise folding by choosing as large a box or drawer as possible. Use an acid-free box or line the box or drawer with metal foil or melinex (Regd, TM) to prevent acids in the cardboard or wood from reaching the item(s). Line with several layers of acid-free tissue paper (available from stationers) leaving flaps of tissue all round to fold over the top. Place rolls of tissue in any folds to stop hard creases forming and place tissue between layers of any one item and between items: decoration should be on the outside of any fold. Place tissue over the top layer and fold over the flaps of the lining tissue.

GLOSSARY (General Decoration, costume, fabric and sewing terms)

Ayrshire embroidery/Ayrshire work In the late 18th - early 19th centuries this was tambour work on white muslin, not the work usually associated with the name which developed in the 1820s.

Baroque A bold design style with a strong sense of movement characterised, in embroidery and lace, by large flowers, leaves and fruits, often of an exotic nature, carried on undulating or scrolling stems sometimes interwoven with decorated ribbons or strapwork.

Bizarre A term coined in recent years for the designs of a group of late 17th - early18th century baroque textiles in which strange geometric shapes are juxtaposed with exotic flowers, fruit and architectural motifs in different relative proportions from real life. Larger shapes are also filled with geometric and floral patterns; there is a strong sense of asymmetry and often odd colour contrasts.

Bobbin lace Any hand-made lace made with a multitude of threads each carried on a bobbin; the bobbins are manipulated to cross and twist the threads together to create the lace fabric.

Brussels bobbin lace A bobbin lace in which small areas or motifs are made separately and subsequently joined to complete an item.

Buffon/buffont A voluminous handkerchief worn puffed up under the chin.

Calico/calicot Originally a cotton fabric from Calcutta, India, but used generally for fine cottons or some cotton/linen mixes but less fine than muslin.

Cambric Originally a fine linen fabric from Cambrai in Flanders but used generally for fine linens or even, in the 19th century, for cottons.

Cartouche A decorative frame formed by various curved shapes.

Chemise The main female knee-length undergarment, usually of linen, sometimes cotton in the 18th century and based on a T-shape with a cut-out neckline: also called a shift.

Chintz A term usually used for glazed printed or painted cotton cloths with oriental designs originally imported from India.

Dorset button Any of several types of button made particularly in Dorset, including fabric-covered metal rings, rings covered with diametrally-wound threads in a wheel pattern, conical padded buttons, etc.

Dresden lace Name coined in the 19th century for extremely fine whitework including a wide variety of drawn-thread stitches; the finest examples were made in Dresden or the surrounding area of Saxony in the 18th century.

Fichu – in Webster's – *neckerchief - a kind of ornamental three-cornered cape, usually of lace muslin or silk, worn by women as a covering for the shoulders and sometimes for the head* – not in general use in English in the 18th century but occurs under the spelling 'fishooe' among others in Fanny Jarvis's accounts (p103).

Filet work/net A hand-made square-meshed net with a knot at each corner of the meshes.

Gauze A fine open fabric in which twisted warps hold the weft.

Gown The English term for a woman's full-length main garment, used interchangeably with the French term 'robe'.

Half-Handkerchief A triangular piece of fabric formed by cutting a square in half diagonally and used like a handkerchief.

Handkerchief A square of fabric often folded in half diagonally and draped around the neck and shoulders.

Holland Very fine linen fabric from the Low Countries.

Kerchief Alternative name for a handkerchief.

Lawn Originally a fine, plain-weave linen fabric, and used here with that meaning, but often used for fine cotton fabrics.

Lappet A hanging piece or streamer: a pair of lappets was commonly attached to the back or sides of a cap.

Mechlin bobbin lace A very fine bobbin lace worked in long lengths and incorporating a thick thread outlining the motifs.

Modesty piece/frill A frill of lace or other fine fabric standing up from the front edge of a woman's neckline partly filling the décolletage.

Muslin Fine, plain-weave cottons varying from very soft, open-weave fabrics to slightly firmer, more closely-woven fabrics.

Needlepoint/needlepoint lace Any lace made by hand solely with a needle and thread. The basic stitch is usually a buttonhole stitch but both the stitch and the way stitches interlink can be varied to give different effects.

Neo-classical A style inspired by ancient Greek and Roman artefacts characterised, in women's dress, by a high waist, slim line and flowing drapery and, in decoration, by bands of repeated, symmetrical motifs or simple, repetitive, linear decoration. Certain motifs, such as the Greek key and spiral designs, are particularly common.

Open robe A robe with a skirt that is open down the front to reveal a petticoat.

Pocket handkerchief Term commonly used in the 18th century for a small handkerchief used for mopping the brow etc.

Point de Dresde/Point de Saxe French terms for Dresden lace.

Polonaise A dress style in which the skirt of the robe is bunched up over the hips by any one of various means.

Pounce A powder used for dusting through holes along lines in a design to transfer the design to an underlying medium.

Robe The French term for a woman's full-length main garment, used interchangeably with the English term 'gown'.

Rococo A light version of the baroque style characterised, in embroidery and lace, by leafy, floral designs with scrolling and branching stems and tendrils, asymmetry and ornamental detail such as cartouches and ribbons filled with filling stitches.

Selvedge The firm longitudinal edge of a woven fabric.

Shawl The late-18th/early-19th century term for a rectangle of fabric of much greater length than width now more usually called a stole.

Shift An alternative name for a chemise.

Stays The 18th century term for a corset.

Stomacher A roughly triangular piece of fabric, often stiffened and decorated, used to fill the gap between the front edges of the bodice of an 18th century robe.

Strapwork Decorative bands or ribbons in a design.

Tambour frame (from the French 'tambour' for drum) A circular frame for stretching fabric for embroidering; particularly used for chain stitch worked with a hooked needle.

Tambour hook Name used for a hooked needle for 'tambouring' i.e. creating chain stitches on a fabric: it has a pointed tip for piercing the fabric.

Tucker A frill of lace or other fabric around the neckline of a gown, often attached to the chemise.

Valenciennes bobbin lace A very fine bobbin lace worked in long lengths: unlike Mechlin lace it has no thick threads outlining motifs.

Van-Dycked/ing A term used to describe a pointed or scalloped edging after the artist Anthony van Dyck whose early 17th century portraits show many edgings of this character.

SELECT BIBLIOGRAPHY

Arnold, J, *Patterns of Fashion I,* Macmillan, 1972

Ashelford, J, *The Art of Dress 1500-1914,* National Trust Enterprises Ltd., 1996

Baker, J. M. *The Moravians:an alternative perspective on whitework embroidery 1780-1850,* M A thesis held in the Winchester School of Art (Southampton University) Library

Bower, H, *Textiles at Temple Newsam,* Leeds Arts collection Fund, 2000

Bradfield, N, *Costume in Detail, Women's dress 1730-1930,* Harrap, 1981

Buck, A, *Dress in Eighteenth-Century England,* Batsford, 1979

Burman, B & Denbo, S, *Pockets of History,* 2007

Burton, A, *The Rise and Fall of King Cotton,* British Broadcasting Corpn, 1984

Butt, J & Ponting, K (Eds), *Scottish Textile History,* Aberdeen Univ. Press, 1987

Byrde, P, *Jane Austen Fashion: Fashion and Needlework in the works of Jane Austen,* Excellent Press, 1999

Campbell, R, *The London Tradesman, 1747 (Reprint),* David & Charles, 1969

Clabburn, P, *The Needleworker's Dictionary,* Macmillan, 1976

Colby, A, *Quilting,* Batsford, 1972

Cunnington & Beard, *Dictionary of English Costume,* A and C Black, 1976

Cunnington, C W & P, *Handbook of English Costume in the 18th Century,* Faber, 1964

Cunnington, C W & P, *A Picture History of English Costume,* Vista Books, 1960

Fangel, E, Winckler, I & Madsen, A W, *Danish Pulled Thread Embroidery,* Dover, 1977

Davis, D, *A History of Shopping,* Routledge & K. Paul, 1966

Diderot, D & d'Alembert, J L, *Encyclopédie ou Dictionnaire raisonné des Sciences, des Arts et des Métiers,* 1751

Foster, V, *Bags and Purses, (Costume Accessories Series),* Batsford, 1982

Hammond, IL&B, *The Skilled Labourer, 1760-1832*

Holland, V, *Hand Coloured Fashion Plates 1770-1899,* Batsford, 1955

Levey, S M, *Lace: a History,* V&A/ Maney, 1983

Mackenzie, A, *Embroideries from Snowshill,* National Trust Enterprises Ltd., 2004

Mackrell, A, *Shawls, Stoles and Scarves, (Costume Accessories Series),* Batsford, 1986

Marsh, G, *18th Century Embroidery Techniques,* Guild of Master Craftsmen Publications Ltd., 2006

Moore, D L, *Fashion through Fashion Plates, 1770-1970,* Ward Lock, 1971

Parker, R, *The Subversive Stitch: Embroidery and the making of the feminine,* Women's Press Ltd., 1984

Ribeiro, A & Cumming, V, *A Visual History of Costume,* Batsford, 1989

Ribeiro, A, *A Visual History of Costume: the 18th Century,* Batsford, 1983

Rose, M B (Ed), *The Lancashire Cotton Industry: A History since 1700,* Lancashire County Books, 1996

Rothstein, N (Ed), *A Lady of Fashion: Barbara Johnson's Album of Styles and Fabrics,* Thames and Hudson/ V&A, 1987

Rothstein, N, *Silk Designs of the Eighteenth Century,* Thames & Hudson, 1990

Scheuer, N & Maeder, E, *Art of the Embroiderer by Charles Germain de Saint-Aubin, Designer to the King, 1770,* Los Angeles County Museum of Art/ D R Godine, 1983

Swain, M, *The Flowerers: the Story of Ayrshire Needlework,* W&R Chambers, 1955

Swain, M, *Scottish Embroidery, Medieval to Modern,* Batsford, 1986

Swain, M, *Ayrshire and other Whitework,* Shire, 1982

Swain, M, *Historical Needlework: a study of Influences in Scotland and Northern England,* Barrie & Jenkins, 1970

Symmonds, M & Preece, L, *Needlework through the Ages,* Hodder & Stoughton, 1928

Toomer, H, *Antique Lace: Identifying Types and Techniques,* Schiffer, 2001

Tozer, J & Levitt, S, *Fabric and Society: A Century of People and their Clothes, 1770-1870,* Laura Ashley

Wark, E, *Drawn Fabric Embroidery,* Batsford, 1979

Waugh, N, *The Cut of Men's Clothes, 1600-1900,* Theatre Arts Books, 1964

Waugh, N, *The Cut of Women's Clothes, 1600-1930,* Faber & Faber, 1968

Museum publications

Los Angeles County Museum of Art, *An Elegant Art: Fashion and Fantasy in the Eighteenth Century,* 1983

Musées et Monuments de France (Arrizoli-Clémentel, P), *The Textile Museum, Lyons,* 1990

National Museums and Galleries on Merseyside (Rushton, P), *18th Century Costume in the National Museums and Galleries on Merseyside,* 1999

National Portrait Gallery (Ribeiro, A), *The Gallery of Fashion,* 2000

Staatliche Kunstsammlungen Dresden kunstgewerbemuseum (Bleckwenn, R), *Dresdner Spitzen – Point de Saxe,* 2000

The Colonial Williamsburg Foundation
(Baumgarten, L), *What Clothes Reveal*, 2002
The Kyoto Costume Institute, *Revolution in Fashion, 1715-1815*, Abbeville Press, 1989
The Royal School of Needlework, (Synge, L, Ed.) *Book of Needlework and Embroidery*, 1986
V&A, *Four Hundred Years of Fashion*, Collins, 1984
V&A (Hart, A & North, S), *Historical fashion in Detail: the 17th and 18th Centuries*, 1998
V&A (Wardle, P), *Guide to English Embroidery*, 1970

Articles in 'Costume', the Journal of
The Costume Society

Adams, S, *Purchases from the Parsonage: observations on Bath Dress and Reactive Shopping by the Penrose Family, 1766-1767*, No.39, 2005
Buck, A & Matthews, H, *Pocket Guides to Fashion*, No.18, 1984
Ehrman, E, *Dressing well in Old age: the clothing accounts of Martha Dodson, 1746-1765*, No.40, 2006
Garry, M A, *'After they went I worked': Mrs. Larpent and her Needlework, 1790-1800*, No.39, 2005
Godman, M, *A Georgian Lady's Personal Accounts*, No.25, 1991
Hayden, P, *Elizabeth Jervis's Clothing*, No.22, 1988
Hunter, J, *The Paisley Textile Industry, 1695-1830*, No.10 1976
Llewellwyn, S, *'Inventory of her Grace's Things, 1747 – The Dress Inventory of Mary Churchill, 2nd Duchess of Montagu'*, No.31, 1997
Sanderson, E, *The Edinburgh Milliners*, No.20, 1986

Other Costume Society publications with articles on 18th century dress: Nos. 6, 17, 24, 26, 32, 33, 35, 36
The So-called Age of Elegance – *1970 Costume Society Conference*
'Strata of Society' – *1973 Costume Society Conference*
Lens, B, *'The Exact Dress of the Head, 1725-6' Reprint*

Articles in 'Textile History'
Thunder, M, *'Object Lesson: Designs and Clients for Embroidered Dress'* No.37, May 2006

PUBLIC COLLECTIONS CONTAINING WHITEWORKED ACCESSORIES AND RELATED MATERIAL

Most good museum costume collections in the UK contain some whiteworked accessories. The list given under 'Acknowledgments' indicates some of these but is by no means exhaustive: it is always worth asking at your local museum. One collection not listed, including important archive material, is: Fulneck Moravian Museum, Pudsey, Leeds. Continental collections also contain examples, particularly the Kunstgewerbemuseums at Dresden and Hamburg and the Textilmuseum at St. Gallen, Switzerland. Costume collections often also contain original fashion magazines, plates and/or other documentary material while these can also be found in reference libraries, both local authority and university. The staff of such institutions have invariably been helpful in suggesting material for study, retrieving it from store and generally facilitating research.

ACCESSORY AND EMBROIDERY PATTERNS TO BE FOUND IN THIS WORK

Patterns in this work
Aprons: pp 136, 137
Kerchiefs: pp140, 146, 150
Shawl: p98
Sleeve ruffles: pp 155, 163
Neck ruffle: p167
Waistcoats: pp 113, 118
Embroidery: pp 9, 75, 85, 92, 94, 99

INDEX

In the index, references are indicated as follows: text - page nos. in standard type; captions - page nos. in italics; plates - nos. in italics